ENGLISH U.S.A. Every Day

A Fun ESL Guide to American Culture and Language

by Dr. Gilda Martínez-Alba

BARRON'S

Acknowledgments

I would like to thank Joe and Elaine Czarnecki for their ongoing support and friendship.

Get access to the downloadable audio dialogues for English USA Every Day at:

http://barronsbooks.com/media/eue2175/

Published by Barron's Educational Series, Inc.

750 Third Avenue

New York, NY 10017

www.barronseduc.com

ISBN: 978-1-4380-0970-4

Library of Congress Catalog Card No.: 2017028397

Library of Congress Cataloging-in-Publication Data

Names: Martínez-Alba, Gilda author.

Title: English U.S.A. Every Day / by Dr. Gilda Martínez-Alba.

Description: New York, NY : Kaplan, Inc., 2017. |

Includes index.

Identifiers: LCCN 2017028397 | ISBN 9781438009704

Subjects: LCSH: English language--Textbooks for foreign speakers. | English language--Grammar--Problems, exercises, etc. | English language--Terms and phrases. | English language--Spoken English--United States.

Classification: LCC PE1128.M35295 2017 | DDC 428.2/4--dc23 LC record available at https://lccn.loc.gov/2017028397

9 8 7 6 5 4 3 2

Barron's Educational Series, Inc. print books are available at special quantity discounts to use for sales promotions, employee premiums, or educational purposes. For more information or to purchase books, please call the Simon & Schuster special sales department at 866-506-1949.

Table of Contents

PART TWO: BEING SOCIAL

Introduction

The Intended Audience and Purpose of This Book

Welcome to this journey for intermediate English learners! You will learn new vocabulary and idioms so that by the time you finish this book, you will sound more like a native English speaker and will more easily understand your friends and coworkers. Each chapter will not only help you with vocabulary and idioms but will also teach you interesting topics related to living in the United States.

This book can be used by teachers in a classroom setting or by self-learners at home. The answers to the practice exercises are located at the end of the book, so you can check to see if you are correct as you go along. There are also activities in each chapter to reinforce what you have learned. For example, these activities include the following:

- DIALOGUE
- STOP AND THINK
- WRITE IT DOWN
- MATCHING
- CROSSWORD
- IDIOMS
- STORY TIME

This makes it easy to follow along throughout the entire book. As each chapter progresses, you will see that the vocabulary and idioms are used more than once to give you time to practice and remember them. There is downloadable audio for you to listen to during the dialogue activities. It might be interesting for you to practice the dialogues with a friend —see if you can say the sentences the way you hear them.

It will help you if you use the vocabulary and idioms that you are learning in the book during your everyday interactions as soon as you can. You will get used to using the words, and they will eventually come naturally to you during conversations. After a while, you will not have to think about their meaning because you will remember them from plenty of practice. Remember: practice makes perfect! Hopefully, you will want to go out and practice what you learn in this book so you can perfect your skills. I hope you have as much fun reading this book and completing the activities as I have had writing it. Now let's get started!

Get access to the downloadable audio dialogues for
English USA Every Day at:

http://barronsbooks.com/media/eue2175/

PART ONE
THE BASICS

CHAPTER 1

American Culture

After reading this chapter, you should know more about . . .

- **The U.S. population**
- **Dos and don'ts in American culture**
- **American values**
- **Vocabulary relating to the United States, such as the following:**
    - Society
    - Multiculturalism
    - Norm
    - Culture shock
    - Culture vulture

Who Lives in the United States?

Did you know that there are more than 300,000,000 people living in the United States? See the following example of a conversation or dialogue about the population. You can listen to the audio online, too.

DIALOGUE 1

Juan: In the United States about 18 percent of the people are Hispanic or Latino.

Sofia: Really? That's interesting, because it seems like there are more Spanish-speaking people than that.

Juan: Maybe that's because we live in an area with a higher percentage?

Sofia: Yes, San Diego, California, has a large Hispanic or Latino population.

Juan: I'll look it up on my phone to find out.

Sofia: That's a good idea.

Juan: On the United States Census Bureau website it says that more than 33 percent of people in San Diego are Hispanics.

Sofia: That makes sense. It seems like everywhere in this society I can hear people speaking in Spanish.

Juan: Yes, and there are Latino markets and restaurants everywhere, too.

Sofia: What else did you see on that website?

Juan: In the United States the majority of the people are white. Then there are 13 percent African American, 6 percent Asian, 1 percent American Indian and Alaska Native, 3 percent are two or more races, and 0.2 percent are Native Hawaiian or Pacific Islander. Hispanics, who can be of any race, make up 18 percent of the population. Identifying as Hispanic is declaring your ethnicity, not your race.

Sofia: That's interesting. I thought there was more multiculturalism.

Hispanic: someone who speaks Spanish and/or has ancestors from Spain. Example: She is Hispanic, but she does not speak too much Spanish.

Latino: someone from Latin America (who may or may not have a family history based in Spain). Example: He is a Latino from El Salvador.

United States Census Bureau: an organization that is located in Suitland, Maryland, and collects information about population growth in the United States. Example: The United States Census Bureau sends questions to people around the United States every ten years to find out how the population is changing.

society: a group of people in a community or area. Example: We live in a society that allows you to speak your mind.

majority: a number or percentage that is more than half of a total. Example: The majority of people in the United States are Caucasian (or white).

multiculturalism: having more than one group of people with different beliefs and values. Example: There is plenty of multiculturalism in the United States.

United States Census Bureau

What might you want to learn about from the United States Census Bureau after looking at these quick facts?

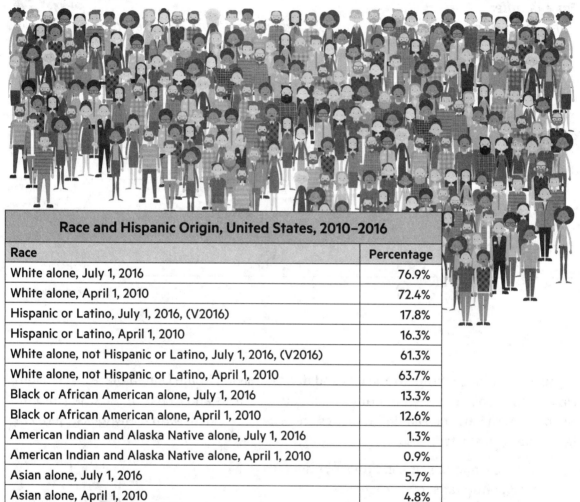

Race and Hispanic Origin, United States, 2010–2016	
Race	**Percentage**
White alone, July 1, 2016	76.9%
White alone, April 1, 2010	72.4%
Hispanic or Latino, July 1, 2016, (V2016)	17.8%
Hispanic or Latino, April 1, 2010	16.3%
White alone, not Hispanic or Latino, July 1, 2016, (V2016)	61.3%
White alone, not Hispanic or Latino, April 1, 2010	63.7%
Black or African American alone, July 1, 2016	13.3%
Black or African American alone, April 1, 2010	12.6%
American Indian and Alaska Native alone, July 1, 2016	1.3%
American Indian and Alaska Native alone, April 1, 2010	0.9%
Asian alone, July 1, 2016	5.7%
Asian alone, April 1, 2010	4.8%

Source: United States Census Bureau. Available at https://www.census.gov/quickfacts/table/PST045215/00.

The United States Census Bureau also has videos that you can view to learn more about who is living in the United States and what the trends are.

The United States Census Bureau also has a mobile app called Census PoP Quiz for Android and iPhone that lets you take a quiz about U.S. facts. For example, did you know the percentage of people who walk in New York? How many people make between $50,000 and $75,000 in St. Petersburg, Florida? How many women have doctoral degrees in Sacramento, California? You can find out the answers through the mobile app quiz. You can also find out the answers through their website. It has so much interesting information to check out!

trend: the direction something is going in, such as a growing Latino population. Example: A trend that can be noticed in the United States is the growing obesity problem.

mobile app: a software application on your phone or tablet. Example: I have too many mobile apps on my phone, so I ran out of space to add any more.

Look up what populations are in your area and write some facts about them here.

For example:
I am going to find out how many people make more than $100,000 a year in San Diego.

_____

_____

_____

_____

_____

_____

_____

(Answers will vary.)

Dos and Don'ts

If you want to find out about the dos and don'ts of living in the United States, you might want to look online for that information. If you type "Dos and Don'ts in the USA" into the Google search bar, you will find websites and YouTube videos with many ideas. Here are a few to get you started:

- Don't change the air conditioner or heater's temperature at someone's house.
- Don't burp or pass gas in public, or do so very discreetly.
- Don't throw trash on the ground.
- Don't talk about religion or politics, in order to avoid conflict.
- Do provide a tip for service of between 15 percent and 20 percent.
- Do use traditional systems of weights and measures, not the metric system.
- Do provide people with personal space.
- Do sneeze or cough into your elbow, not your hands.

Let's see how much you know. The following sentences are some typical dos and don'ts about life in the United States. Write TRUE or FALSE next to the following sentences. When you've finished, check the answer key at the end of the book to see how many you answered correctly.

_____ **1.** You should tip people for service in restaurants.

_____ **2.** Most people wear fancy clothes when they go out.

_____ **3.** You should visit someone only after they agree to a date and time for you to come over.

_____ **4.** You should greet people by saying hello and using eye contact.

_____ **5.** There is a set time for taking a nap every day.

_____ **6.** Many Americans have a first and middle name.

_____ **7.** You can cross the street only at designated points.

_____ **8.** It is polite to ask people their age.

_____ **9.** It is common to ask people how much money they make.

_____ **10.** Smoking is not allowed in most places.

(Answers are on page 247.)

DIALOGUE 2

Listen to the following dialogue, and notice how Juan and Sofia talk about a few dos and don'ts of living in the United States.

Sofia: Hi Juan! I was thinking of coming over to your house later?

Juan: Sure, that would be fun.

Sofia: Isn't it interesting that Americans need to schedule times to meet? They don't just come to each other's houses.

Juan: Yeah, but you know you can come to my house anytime.

Sofia: Thanks, Juan! I like that I can talk to you about the dos and don'ts that are new to me.

Juan: One that was new to me was no nap time. That was very sad news.

Sofia: I know what you mean. I miss nap time. It's just not the norm here.

Juan: A virtuous one, though, is that people don't smoke in most public places.

Sofia: I love that!

Juan: It's also pretty remarkable how most Americans have a first and middle name.

schedule: a plan to take place at a certain time. Example: He likes to follow his schedule closely to make sure he gets to his meetings on time.

norm: something common or usual. Example: It is the norm for people to try to get to places on time in the United States.

virtuous: being of high moral standards. Example: She can seem overly virtuous because she always tries to be perfect.

remarkable: something you would notice. Example: The work she has done is remarkable because it is very detailed and organized.

How many dos and don'ts did Juan and Sofia talk about? Think about those and the ones discussed before and write down some dos and don'ts you may follow in your everyday life. If you would like more ideas, look on the About Travel website to find out more: *http://usatravel.about.com/od/Plan-Your-Trip/tp/Dos-And-Donts-For-USA-Travel.htm.* Later, talk to a friend about them.

_____

_____

_____

_____

_____

(Answers will vary.)

Vocabulary Crossword

Complete the crossword below using the vocabulary you just learned.

ACROSS

2. The U.S. community is very large.
6. There are different groups of people with different beliefs in the U.S.
7. The U.S. population is growing.
8. My grandparents are from Spain.

DOWN

1. I am from South America.
2. Let's figure out a time to get together.
3. I hope to have high moral standards.
4. Everyone dresses this way in the U.S.
5. There are mostly English speakers in the U.S.

(Answers are on page 247.)

VOCABULARY CHECK

Use the following words in a sentence.

For example:

schedule: *I would like to schedule a time to talk with you.*

norm: ____

____

multiculturalism: ____

____

Latino: ____

____

remarkable: ____

____

trend: ____

____

majority: ____

____

Hispanic: ____

____

society: ____

____

virtuous: ____

____

(Answers will vary.)

Idioms Related to American Culture

Idioms are phrases that do not make sense when you translate them into your native language but are used by Americans all of the time. Therefore, it is a good idea to learn the meaning of these idioms in order to understand native English speakers more easily.

as American as apple pie	something that is very American. (Apple pie is considered to be a very American dessert.)
Uncle Sam	another way to say the American government.
don't tread on me	do not take advantage of me. (This saying originated during the American Revolution with an image of a coiled rattlesnake, meaning that if you stepped on the snake [the colonies], it would bite you.)
close but no cigar	you were very close to winning. (There used to be cigars given as prizes at American carnivals if you won a game. If you almost won, they may have said, "Close but no cigar.")
cut to the chase	tell the main point of the story. (American silent movies sometimes had scenes that were too long, so the director may have said to cut some parts to get to the action—or the chase.)
jump the gun	do something too quickly. (Track and field races in the United States are sometimes started with a gun shot. If you started before the gun shot, you have jumped the gun.)
get on the bandwagon	join the group. (A bandwagon was the wagon that carried the circus band. The word was first used in the United States in the nineteenth century.)

Culture Shock

Listen to the next dialogue to hear what Sofia had to say about the culture shock she experienced. As you listen, think about how that may or may not relate to the culture shock you have experienced.

DIALOGUE 3

Juan: Did you know that the United States is one of the most **diverse** countries in the world?

Sofia: I thought you said that the majority of the people in the United States are white, so there isn't that much multiculturalism.

Juan: I did say that the majority of the people are white, but the white population is diverse, too. There are, for example, Italians, Germans, Russians, and Jewish people who are white. And all of them are from very different cultures.

Sofia: So, they still get **culture shock**?

Juan: What do you mean?

Sofia: What kinds of culture shock do those people experience in America?

Juan: It depends on where they are from. Some of the diverse people in the United States are born in the United States. They **probably** don't experience culture shock.

Sofia: How come when I moved from Miami, Florida, to Cleveland, Ohio, I experienced culture shock then?

Juan: Oh, I see what you mean. I can see that coming from Miami, **which** has many Latinos, to Cleveland, where there are very few Latinos, could create culture shock. Or even moving from a farming area to a city could create culture shock. I guess culture shock can happen to anyone who goes to a place that is different from where they're used to living!

Sofia: Yeah. Maybe people who come from other countries experience culture shock more **significantly**, but even moving within the United States can **provide** culture shock.

diverse: being different from each other. Example: We live in a diverse country.

culture shock: experiencing a different way of doing things that is surprising. Example: You might experience culture shock when you move to another part of the country.

probably: maybe, likely, possibly. Example: He will probably make it to the movies on time if he leaves work a little early.

which: a word that leads to additional information. Example: She likes to eat pie, which is why she enjoys finding new bakeries.

significantly: in a very important and noticeable way. Example: Her decision on whether to marry him will significantly change his thoughts about her.

provide: to give. Example: He will provide her with the answers after lunch.

Read this story about Sofia's day, and answer the questions that follow.

Sofia grew up in Miami, Florida. She was used to being around many Latinos, especially people from Cuba. She enjoyed going to eat typical Cuban foods, such as white rice, black beans, pork, and plantains. She took them for granted.

She had no idea that when she moved to Cleveland, Ohio, which was about 1,000 miles away, she would miss Cuban food. There were no Cuban restaurants, and she was very surprised to find out that the grocery store had only one section for Hispanic food. Back in Miami, grocery stores had Hispanic food in every aisle. She also experienced cold weather for the first time. Her new friends told her to use layers, meaning she should put on lots of clothes. She felt very uncomfortable with layers. Even though she missed Cuban food and disliked the cold, she really liked her new job and friends. This helped her feel happy in her new city.

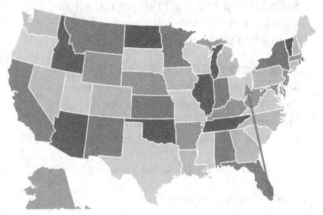

1. Why did Sofia miss Miami?
   - **A.** She did not like her new job.
   - **B.** She wanted to go to school in Miami.
   - **C.** She could not find Cuban food.
   - **D.** She missed her old friends.

2. How often did Sofia go to the grocery store?
   - **A.** Every day
   - **B.** Two times a week
   - **C.** Once a month
   - **D.** The story did not say how often she went to the grocery store.

3. What helped Sofia feel better when she moved?
   - **A.** Her new friends
   - **B.** Her new house
   - **C.** Her old friends
   - **D.** Her new clothes

4. Did Sofia experience culture shock?
   - **A.** Yes
   - **B.** No
   - **C.** The story did not talk about culture shock.

5. How far is Cleveland from Miami?
   - **A.** About 1,000 miles
   - **B.** About 10,000 miles
   - **C.** About 100,000 miles
   - **D.** None of the above

(Answers are on page 247.)

WRITE IT DOWN

Now it is your turn to write a story. What is the most significant culture shock you have experienced? Why do you think you felt that way? Explain the story below, and later tell a friend about it. Have them tell you their culture shock story, too.

_____

_____

_____

_____

_____

_____

(Answers will vary.)

Culture Vulture

Are you a culture vulture? A culture vulture is someone who is very interested in the arts. If you are in the Washington, D.C. area, it is easy to be a culture vulture because there is always a show or new theater production to see. Some are created by Latinos, since there is a Latino population in that area. Sofia is not quite a culture vulture; she is close but no cigar. She probably goes to a show every few months, but you have to go see the arts more than that to be seen as a culture vulture.

WRITE IT DOWN

What percentage of U.S. society is a culture vulture? It is not the norm. In other words, there is not a significant number of people who are culture vultures. Let's cut to the chase, or get to the point: are you a culture vulture? If you are, write down what kinds of art or shows you like to see. If you are not, write down what you like to do for fun after you answer the questions.

1. What is a culture vulture?

_____

2. Is Sofia a culture vulture?

_____

3. Are you a culture vulture?

_____

4. Write down what you like to do for fun. Is it going to see art shows or going to the theater? Or do you like going out to eat?

_____

_____

_____

_____

_____

_____

(Answers are on page 247.)

MATCHING

Match the following words to their definitions.

A. Hispanic
B. Latino
C. United States Census Bureau
D. Majority
E. Multiculturalism
F. Trend
G. Mobile app
H. Schedule
I. Norm
J. Remarkable
K. Diverse
L. Culture shock
M. Culture vulture
N. Significantly

1. _____ more than one group of people with different beliefs and values

2. _____ the direction something is going in, such as a growing Latino population

3. _____ a plan to take place at a certain time

4. _____ something you would notice

5. _____ someone who speaks Spanish and/or has ancestors from Spain

6. _____ something common or usual

7. _____ experiencing a different way of doing things that is surprising

8. _____ in a very important and noticeable way

9. _____ someone from Latin America

10. _____ this organization is located in Suitland, Maryland, and collects information about population growth in the United States

11. _____ a number or percentage that is more than half of a total

12. _____ a software application on your phone or tablet

13. _____ being different from each other

14. _____ someone who is very interested in the arts

(Answers are on page 247.)

Use the following idioms in a sentence.

as American as apple pie

_____

Uncle Sam

_____

don't tread on me

_____

close but no cigar

_____

cut to the chase

_____

jump the gun

_____

get on the bandwagon

_____

(Answers will vary.)

Chapter Reflection

The following is a summary of what was covered in this chapter, including who lives in the United States and information about the United States Census Bureau, American culture, and culture shock. You should access the United States Census Bureau's website to learn more about population trends in the United States.

Vocabulary

Hispanic

Latino

United States Census Bureau

society

majority

multiculturalism

schedule

norm

virtuous

remarkable

mobile app

diverse

culture shock

probably

which

significantly

provide

trend

Idioms

as American as apple pie

Uncle Sam

don't tread on me

close but no cigar

cut to the chase

jump the gun

get on the bandwagon

Do you remember all of the information we covered in this chapter? If not, go back and review it to make sure you do. Practice the vocabulary and idioms in your conversations, and look for them when you are reading different materials. In what direction do you think the U.S. population trends are going? Visit the United States Census Bureau website to learn more about them. Later, find a friend to talk about the changes that are occurring.

CHAPTER 2

Shopping for Food

After reading this chapter, you should know more about . . .

- **Finding the right store to meet your needs**
- **Organization of grocery stores**
- **Using vocabulary about food shopping, such as the following:**
    - Aisles
    - Butcher
    - Bakery

Finding the Store to Meet Your Needs

Think about what you are interested in buying before going shopping. Some areas have grocery stores everywhere. You can also quickly figure out who generally lives in a neighborhood by the grocery stores you see. For example, if you see many Indian or Asian grocery stores, you can be pretty sure that there is a rather significant Indian or Asian population. However, you might be in what some people call a food desert. This means that there are not many places to buy food. It also means that the small grocery stores you do find are usually expensive and do not have many fruit and vegetable choices. Let's see how Sofia and Juan found grocery stores in their neighborhood in the following dialogue.

DIALOGUE 1

Sofia: I wonder if there's an Asian market in the area.

Juan: Did you try looking on the Yelp app or website? It has places in your area with ratings from customers.

Sofia: I knew there had to be an app for that! There's an app for everything.

Juan: I just found an Asian market on 23rd Street through Yelp.

Sofia: I have been driving around looking for large grocery stores but with no luck. I think I just moved to a food desert.

Juan: That's a problem. However, once you figure out where the grocery stores are, you can plan to go to them when you are in the area.

Sofia: Yes, that's true. It would have been nice to have one within a few minutes of my place though.

Juan: Well, you can get into a routine and go once a week to get everything you need at one time.

Sofia: You're right. Thanks for making me feel better about the food desert.

Yelp: an app and website that gives ratings for restaurants, attractions, and services. Example: Can you please find a restaurant on Yelp for us?

app: an application on your phone. Example: I have an app that helps me find my keys.

Yelp app: an application on your phone that provides you with locations of interest, such as restaurants and stores, and tells you what other people thought of these locations. Example: I downloaded the Yelp app to make it easier to find good restaurants.

ratings: a score for something, such as how many people thought the Asian market on 23rd Street deserved a score of 5 out of a possible 5.

Example: The ratings for that restaurant were pretty bad, so let's go somewhere else.

food desert: an area where there are not many grocery stores. Example: He lives in a food desert, so he has to shop at a place outside of his neighborhood.

however: a word used before mentioning something that is different from or contradicts something just said. Example: She would like to eat there; however, she does not have enough money.

routine: what you do regularly, such as to going to the grocery store once a week. Example: She has a routine of eating dinner at 6 p.m. every day.

What type of grocery store are you looking for? Are you looking for one with ethnic foods? Are you looking for one with organic foods, or maybe a farmer's market? Are you looking for one as close as possible to your home? Look at the following picture of the Yelp website, and think about what you might search for to get what you need.

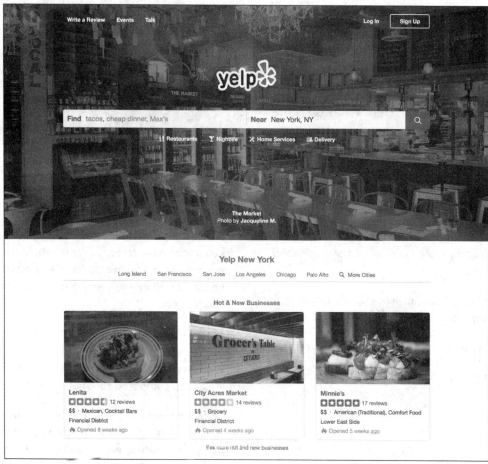

Note: Reprinted with permission from Yelp.com.

Write down a bulleted list of what you want or need from the grocery store. A bulleted list looks like this:

- oranges
- apples
- cheese

(Answers will vary.)

A cheap and organic grocery store can be an **oxymoron**. That means that items that are both cheap and organic are probably not going to be easy to find in a grocery store. You might find a cheap grocery store and another store that has organic food. However, organic grocery stores are usually expensive. Some grocery stores are **pricey** but have many organic **items** and healthy foods. **On the other hand**, some have only organic items at cheaper prices. **Regardless**, you can find what you do have on Yelp. What do Sofia and Juan **suggest**? Let's see in the next dialogue.

DIALOGUE 2

Juan: Now that I am a **vegetarian** it's hard to find grocery stores with all of the vegetables that I like.

Sofia: Well, it sounds like you will be using the Yelp app, too!

Juan: What did we do before we had Yelp?

Sofia: We had to ask people for the answers.

Juan: That's true.

Sofia: It would take longer, though, because you might have to ask several people before finding out the answers. You also wouldn't know how other people felt about that one person's **suggestion**.

Juan: I have found the **Walmart Supercenter** to be my favorite in the area because even though they do not have as many organic choices, they are cheap compared to Whole Foods.

Sofia: I've been to a Walmart Supercenter and agree that they're cheap. They also have other things you might need so you don't have to shop at other stores.

Juan: Some Target stores also sell food and can be cheaper than the **gourmet** or expensive grocery stores.

Sofia: I have noticed that, but always forget about that **option**.

Juan: You have to check it out, but keep in mind that Target might not have all of the food items you need.

Sofia: Thanks!

oxymoron: two things that contradict or are the opposites of each other. Example: Seeing her ex-boyfriend was bittersweet—such an oxymoron!

pricey: when something costs a lot of money. Example: The fruit at Whole Foods is pricey.

items: things, such as food or clothes. Example: He has many items in his grocery cart.

on the other hand: an idiom used to introduce something that means the opposite or a gives a different view than an idea previously mentioned. Example: She would like to eat out; on the other hand, her friend wants to cook.

regardless: no matter what. Example: She would like to go to the party regardless of the weather.

suggest; suggestion: to give advice; an idea. Example: She can suggest some good places

to eat because she has lived in the area a long time.

vegetarian: someone who does not eat meat, fish, or poultry. Example: He became a vegetarian because he thinks killing animals for food is unkind.

Walmart Supercenter: a Walmart store that sells a variety of food items. Example: I go to the Walmart Supercenter for all of my shopping.

gourmet: fancy food that is usually expensive, such as food sold only at high quality food stores. Example: Jasper usually had simple tastes, but every once in a while he wanted something gourmet for dinner.

option: a choice. Example: You have the option of going to the store or staying home.

Idiom and Vocabulary Crossword

Complete the crossword below using the idioms and vocabulary you just learned.

ACROSS

3. This word is used to talk about how something is different.

4. Things such as food or clothes (singular)

7. Give advice or an idea

8. A choice

10. Someone who does not eat meat, fish, or poultry

DOWN

1. Fancy food that is usually expensive

2. Gives you a score for something, such as how many people thought the Asian market on 23rd Street deserved a score of 5

5. No matter what or anyway

6. The Yelp _____ on your phone provides you with locations of interest and tells you what other people thought about them.

8. Two things that contradict or are opposites of each other

9. A food _____ is an area where there are not many grocery stores.

(Answers are on page 247.)

Use five or more of the vocabulary words we have talked about in this chapter to explain what type of grocery store you like to go to and why. Underline the words as you use them. For example:

I like to go to Trader Joe's to buy my food because they have <u>gourmet items</u> and <u>options</u> that are not so <u>pricey</u>. <u>However</u>, sometimes it is just easier to go to the <u>Walmart Supercenter</u> so that I can do all of my shopping in one place. Since I am not a <u>vegetarian</u>, it usually works for me. I have noticed that they don't have my favorite cereal, so my <u>routine</u> is to go there first, and then if I need to, I go to Trader Joe's to finish my shopping.

_____

_____

_____

_____

_____

_____

(Answers will vary.)

Idioms Related to Food

The following idioms are commonly used by native English speakers.

two peas in a pod	two of a kind or very similar
going nuts	going crazy
cold as ice	not a very caring person
icing on the cake	something good that is added to another good thing
cherry on top	something small and special that is added to something else that is also very special
have your cake and eat it too	to have everything you want
cheesy	something that is silly
piece of cake	something that is easy to do
sweet as pie	someone that is very nice
don't bite the hand that feeds you	don't put down the people that support you
don't put all your eggs in one basket	don't risk everything on one plan
like a chicken with its head cut off	acting very distracted or crazy

STOP AND THINK

Fill in the blanks using the idioms you just learned.

1. She is not a warm or kind person; she is as cold as _____ .

2. Juan likes to do some very silly or _____ dance moves when he is shopping.

3. I'm going _____ trying to figure out where all of the grocery stores are located.

4. With the Yelp app it is a _____ of cake to find local grocery stores.

5. The cashier in the grocery store was as sweet as _____ because she got me several coupons to help me save money.

6. Susan got a promotion today, and her husband bought her flowers. Winning $500 on a lottery ticket was just the _____ on the cake.

7. She would like to relax and travel all of the time, but you can't have your _____ and eat it too.

8. When Xavier's boss praised him for his proposal during the meeting, it was the _____ on top of an already great day.

9. You should not talk poorly about your boss, because you don't bite the hand that _____ you.

10. Don't put all your _____ in one basket by putting all of your money into that investment.

11. She ran around like a _____ with its head cut off while planning her wedding.

(Answers are on page 247.)

How did that go? Were you able to fill in the blanks? Let's see how Sofia and Juan use some of the idioms in the next dialogue. As you listen to them, underline them.

DIALOGUE 3

Sofia: Juan, are you doing your cheesy dance moves again?

Juan: You're as cold as ice. How can you not like my moves?

Sofia: I'm just kidding with you.

Juan: We're like two peas in a pod.

Sofia: Yes, but sometimes you drive me nuts. And I'm already going nuts with moving and having to figure everything out.

Juan: But with the Yelp app that is a piece of cake.

Sofia: It is not that easy to figure everything out.

Juan: I know you will figure it all out soon. Plus, you have me, and that is the icing on the cake.

Sofia: Thanks, Juan!

(Answers are on page 247.)

A. App
B. Yelp app
C. Ratings
D. Food desert
E. However
F. Routine
G. Oxymoron
H. Pricey
I. Items
J. Suggest; suggestion
K. Vegetarian
L. Walmart Supercenter
M. Gourmet
N. Option

1. _____ an application on your phone that provides you with locations of interest and tells you what other people thought of the locations

2. _____ an application on your phone

3. _____ a choice

4. _____ a word used to introduce an idea that is different from something previously mentioned

5. _____ two things that contradict or are the opposites of each other

6. _____ things, such as food or clothes

7. _____ someone who does not eat meat, fish, or poultry

8. _____ gives you a score for something, such as how many people thought the Asian market on 23rd Street deserved a score of 5 out of a possible 5

9. _____ a Walmart store that sells lots of food

10. _____ what you do regularly, such as to go to the grocery store once a week

11. _____ when something costs a lot of money

12. _____ to give advice; an idea

13. _____ an area where there are not many grocery stores

14. _____ fancy food that is usually expensive, such as food sold only at high quality food stores

(Answers are on page 247.)

Organization of Grocery Stores

Grocery stores usually have aisles, or rows of shelves with food. As you probably have realized, this makes it easy to see all of the food. Some grocery stores have a butcher you can talk to about getting meat items you might not see in the meat section. For example, you might want to buy a pork tenderloin and only see pork chops. The butcher can tell you if they have any pork tenderloin and can go in the back of the store to get it for you. He might even cut it up for you if it is not yet prepared. Other grocery stores have a bakery where you can get sweet treats, such as cakes and cookies that are usually made in the store. Let's find out about Sofia and Juan's favorite aisles in the following dialogue.

Juan: My favorite section in any grocery store is the **produce** section, where the fruits and vegetables are located.

Sofia: I could have guessed that, considering you're a vegetarian.

Juan: I think of myself as a healthy person.

Sofia: I'm not that healthy. I like to exercise, but my favorite section is the bakery. I love freshly baked cupcakes.

Juan: I like those too. I also like to go down the candy aisle to see if they have anything new.

Sofia: I guess you don't eat that much candy, though, since you're thin.

Juan: Well, I don't eat that much in general.

Sofia: I have to eat five small meals a day; otherwise, I get too hungry.

Juan: That requires planning and organization.

Sofia: Yes, but to me it's worth it. Even if I just eat peanuts and granola bars for a meal, I need to eat my five meals so I don't feel hungry.

Juan: Well, I guess that if you know what you want to buy, you can quickly go down the aisles.

Sofia: That is true. I get through the grocery store pretty fast since I almost always buy the same things.

aisle: a row or lane, such as a row in the grocery store. Example: She went down the candy aisle and picked up three bags of lollipops.

butcher: the person who cuts up the meat and prepares the meat packages. Example: The butcher can tell you if filet mignon is available.

section: part. Example: I would like to go to the frozen foods section to get some ice cream.

bakery: place where sweet treats, such as cakes and cookies, are made. Example: The bakery in that grocery store has many types of pies.

produce: fruits and vegetables. Example: The produce seems like it is not fresh.

What are your favorite aisles or sections in the grocery store? Use three or more of the vocabulary words we just covered. Underline the vocabulary words as you write them. For example:

My favorite sections of the grocery store are the cereal and ethnic <u>aisles</u>. I like the cereal aisle because if I don't feel like cooking, I can always just eat a bowl of cereal. I always make sure I have cereal in my kitchen cabinet. The ethnic section has some of my favorite foods <u>items</u>, such as sweet and sour sauce for chicken. I also like the <u>bakery</u> <u>section</u> because I love sweets.

_____

_____

_____

_____

_____

_____

(Answers will vary.)

Chapter Reflection

The following is a summary of what was covered in this chapter, including how to find a store that has the things you need, idioms related to shopping for food, and why to use Yelp. To practice some of the vocabulary from this chapter, go to a grocery store today and ask someone where the bakery section is located or which aisle has a certain food.

Vocabulary

Yelp	oxymoron	gourmet
app	pricey	option
Yelp app	items	aisle
ratings	regardless	butcher
food desert	suggest; suggestion	section
however	vegetarian	bakery
routine	Walmart Supercenter	produce

Idioms

on the other hand

two peas in a pod

going nuts

cold as ice

icing on the cake

cherry on top

have your cake and eat it too

cheesy

piece of cake

sweet as pie

don't bite the hand that feeds you

don't put all your eggs in one basket

like a chicken with its head cut off

Do you remember all the information we covered in this chapter? If not, go back and review it to make sure you do. Practice the vocabulary and idioms in your conversations, and look for them when you are reading different materials. Use the Yelp app to find a grocery store near you that has good ratings. Then, visit the store and see how many vocabulary words you see written in the store, such as *vegetarian*, *gourmet*, and *aisle* and try to use them in sentences while talking to people in the store.

CHAPTER 3

Cooking

After reading this chapter, you should know more about . . .

- **Working in the kitchen**
- **Following a recipe using a non-metric system**
- **Using vocabulary about cooking, such as the following:**
    - Tablespoon
    - Cup
    - Ounce

Are You Hungry?

If you want to eat healthier, it is a good idea to cook your own food. Many restaurants fry their foods, and they also provide very large portions. If you were to eat out all of the time, it would be easy to gain weight, especially if you eat fast food. What do Juan and Sofia have to say about eating out? Let's find out in the first dialogue.

DIALOGUE 1

Juan: Hey, Sofia, do you want to get something to eat?

Sofia: I'd rather indulge in a home-cooked meal.

Juan: Oh, let's go eat at Ruby Tuesday. You can get your favorite appetizer sampler!

Sofia: I've been eating out too much lately. I just want to eat at home. Maybe I will make some spaghetti. Would you like some? I can make it vegetarian for you.

Juan: That sounds good. Are you going to cook it soon? I'm really hungry.

Sofia: I can get started now, and it should be ready pretty quickly. It doesn't take that long to boil some pasta and heat up some sauce.

Juan: Are you going to cook them in the microwave?

Sofia: No, I'll make them on the stove.

Juan: Do you need any assistance?

Sofia: Feel free to boil the water while I add my secret ingredients to the sauce.

Juan: Okay, I can do that!

---

eat out: go to eat at a restaurant. Example: I want to eat out tonight because I don't feel like cooking.

indulge: have something you want and enjoy, such as a type of food. Example: Let's indulge in a hot fudge sundae.

appetizer sampler: an appetizer is food you order to come out before your main meal at a restaurant, and a sampler usually has three to five different foods on a plate so you can get a few bites of each. Example: She would like to get an appetizer sampler before getting her burger.

vegetarian: a person who does not eat meat, fish, or poultry. Example: He is a vegetarian because he thinks it is the healthiest way to eat.

boil: to heat water until it starts bubbling because it is so hot. Example: You should boil the water before putting in the spaghetti.

microwave: a device that can heat or cook your food using electromagnetic waves. Example: She heated up some hot chocolate in the microwave.

assistance: help. Example: She would like some assistance in understanding the menu.

ingredients: things in a recipe; for example, spaghetti sauce might need salt, garlic, oregano, onions, tomatoes, and cooking wine. Example: If you leave out some of the ingredients, it will not taste right.

What might you want to cook? Or do you prefer to eat out? Write down your opinion here and what you would cook today. For example:

I want to cook meatloaf and potatoes for dinner. I love eating out, but sometimes I am in the mood for something I cook at home.

_____

_____

_____

_____

_____

(Answers will vary.)

Measurements

It is probably a good idea to go out and buy a measuring cup and a set of measuring spoons. This will help you put in the right amount of each ingredient listed in your recipe. A set of measuring cups usually has, from smallest to largest:

¼ cup	½ cup	1 cup
⅓ cup	¾ cup	

Measuring spoons usually include, from smallest to largest:

⅛ teaspoon	½ teaspoon	½ tablespoon
¼ teaspoon	1 teaspoon	1 tablespoon

Go get your measuring spoons and cups so you can start to cook!

Go to *http://www.myrecipes.com/how-to/metric-conversion-charts* to see convenient metric equivalent conversion charts.

Time to Cook

How about we make some salmon salad? That is a quick and healthy meal. All you have to do is cook the salmon and put together the salad. Salmon cooks pretty quickly, so before you know it, you will be eating!

Salmon Salad Recipe
Ingredients (serving for one person)

6-ounce salmon filet
1 tablespoon Italian seasoning (or your favorite seasoning)
3 cups of fresh spinach
⅛ cup dried cranberries
1 tablespoon sliced almonds
¼ cup mangoes
3 tablespoons goat cheese
2 tablespoons balsamic vinegar glaze
1 tablespoon olive oil

Coat the salmon with olive oil and Italian seasoning (or your favorite seasoning). Place 3 cups of spinach in a bowl. Sprinkle the dried cranberries and almonds over the spinach. Cut up the mango into squares and put it along the edges of the bowl. Then sprinkle the goat cheese along the edge. (This keeps the mangoes and goat cheese cool when you put the salmon in the middle of the bowl later on.) Cook the salmon on medium on your stove for about five minutes or until it is cooked the way you like it. Be careful not to overcook it. Finally, place the salmon in the middle of the bowl and put the balsamic vinegar glaze on top. Dinner is ready in 15 minutes!

recipe: a set of instructions for preparing a meal with certain ingredients. Example: I would love to have the recipe for your salmon salad.

serving: a helping of food. Example: That recipe has four servings.

ounce: a weight measurement that is $\frac{1}{16}$ of a pound, or about 28 grams. Example: The steak she ordered weighed 8 ounces.

seasoning: spices, herbs, or salt used to make food flavorful. Example: Cooking food without any seasoning is not a good idea.

mango: a tropical fruit that can be red, green, or yellow/orange on the outside and is orange on the inside. Example: The best time of year to buy mangoes is in the summer.

glaze: a syrup or thick liquid. Example: She made a glaze to go on top of the salmon.

coat: to cover (a coat can also be worn by people when it is cold outside). Example: He coated the salmon with seasoning before cooking it.

sprinkle: to pour very little and lightly. Example: She should sprinkle some more salt on the chicken because it doesn't have enough on it.

edge: along the border of something. Example: Sometimes restaurants will put parsley on the edge of your plate as a decoration to make your food look nice.

overcook: to cook too long, making the food dry. Example: If you overcook food, it usually doesn't taste very good.

STOP AND THINK

Use the following vocabulary words in a sentence.

eat out

_____

_____

indulge

_____

_____

boil

_____

_____

microwave

_____

_____

assistance

_____

_____

ingredients

_____

_____

(Answers will vary.)

Read this story about Sofia's cooking, and answer the questions that follow.

Some days in the kitchen are good, and some are bad. Sofia was on a roll *the other day when she made pumpkin soup as an appetizer, chicken and rice as the main meal, and then chocolate cake for dessert. Not only did she* cook up a storm, *but everything was* done to a T. *However, that isn't always the case in the kitchen. Last week she tried to make a simple scrambled egg and overcooked it. Then she tried to make some toast and burned that, too. It is like she* jumped out of the fire and into the frying pan. *Well, at least she knew that it was just a bad cooking day and not a problem where there were* too many cooks in the kitchen. *Fortunately, she knows that happens to everyone, so she has not given up cooking.*

The words in blue in the story are idioms. Can you guess what they mean?

1. On a roll

    A. Rolling something

    B. Doing well

2. Cook up a storm

    A. Cooking many things

    B. Getting ready for bad weather

3. Done to a T

    A. Cooked perfectly

    B. Cooked in the shape of a T

4. Jumped out of the fire and into the frying pan

    A. Everything was hot

    B. Went from a bad thing to an even worse thing

5. Too many cooks in the kitchen

    A. Several people cooking

    B. When too many people help, it can turn out to be a problem

(Answers are on page 247.)

Juan cooks sometimes, too. Let's see what he is getting ready to do in the kitchen in the following dialogue. As you follow along, underline the vocabulary words and idioms you have learned in this chapter.

Juan: I think I'd like to make my own recipe for **ratatouille**.

Sofia: Did you go shopping already?

Juan: Yes, but if you have any **leftover** spinach or goat cheese, I can use them.

Sofia: I have an **abundance** of spinach but not goat cheese. I bought one of the bigger **containers** thinking I might cook some another day. You can use it though.

Juan: Great! I can use that to go along with the zucchini, tomatoes, onions, and kale.

Sofia: What are you going to use for seasoning?

Juan: I was thinking of using some Italian seasoning with salt, garlic, onions, and oregano. I think it tastes pretty good.

Sofia: Yes, I use Italian seasoning sometimes. I like it. What other ingredients will you add?

Juan: Olive oil, cooking wine, and I think that is it.

Sofia: Well, that's the nice thing about **creating** your own recipe. You can stop adding in things whenever you want.

Juan: Soon we will indulge in my delicious meal. I won't be cooking up a storm, but I hope you like it.

Sofia: I hope you make extra so that we can have leftovers tomorrow.

Juan: I plan on eating this for a few days, so yes, I am making enough for leftovers.

Sofia: Well, it looks like you **know your way around the kitchen**.

(Answers are on page 247.)

ratatouille: a vegetarian recipe that is made up of several vegetables, such as onions, eggplant, zucchini, and peppers. Example: When she went on a diet she made ratatouille quite often.

leftover: something that is left unused or unconsumed. Example: If you have plenty of leftovers, you won't have to cook the next day.

abundance: a lot, plenty. Example: She always makes an abundance of food to last her the week.

container: a box or place to store something in, such as the plastic box you can buy spinach in. Example: He recycles all of the plastic containers.

creating: making. Example: She will be creating a new recipe for the turkey.

know your way around the kitchen: an idiom meaning a person knows how to cook. Example: You make the best dinners—you clearly know your way around the kitchen.

WRITE IT DOWN

Do you ever try to cook for the entire week at once? Explain why or why not. If you were to cook for the whole week, what would you make? Later, ask a friend if he or she sometimes cooks for the whole week.

_____

_____

_____

_____

_____

(Answers will vary.)

MATCHING

Match the following words to their definitions.

A. recipe

B. serving

C. ounce

D. seasoning

E. mango

F. glaze

G. coat

H. sprinkle

I. edge

J. overcook

1. _____ to pour very little and lightly

2. _____ a weight measurement totaling $\frac{1}{16}$ of a pound

3. _____ to cover

4. _____ spices, herbs, or salt used to make food flavorful

5. _____ cook too long, making the food dry

6. _____ a syrup or thick liquid

7. _____ a tropical fruit that is usually red, green, and yellow/orange on the outside and orange on the inside

8. _____ along the border of something

9. _____ a helping of food

10. _____ a set of instructions for preparing a meal with certain ingredients

(Answers are on page 247.)

Idioms Related to Cooking

Read the following idioms and think about if there are any similar idioms in your native language. It can be fun to compare idioms between languages!

good to the last drop	every bit of it was tasty
hats off to the chef	a way to say that the chef did a great job
stirring the pot	creating problems
shaken up	getting nervous because of something that happened
toasty	feeling warm
a toast	raising a glass to say something to honor someone or something
bun in the oven	a way to say someone is pregnant
nuke it	to microwave something
if you can't take the heat, stay out of the kitchen	if something is too hard or stressful for you, stop trying to do it

WRITE IT DOWN

Which of these idioms are new to you? Write a short story using three or more of the idioms. Use a separate sheet of paper if necessary.

_____

_____

_____

_____

_____

_____

(Answers will vary.)

Idiom Crossword

Complete the crossword below using the idioms you just learned.

ACROSS

1. You can _____ it for 3 minutes to make it very hot.

5. He is always making problems for people. He is always _____ the pot.

7. He was _____ up after that car accident.

8. Let's make a _____ to celebrate her new job.

DOWN

2. Since that is too hard for you, if you can't take the heat stay out of the _____.

3. I loved that meal. That was good to the last _____.

4. The chef did fantastic. _____ off to the chef.

6. It feels nice and _____ in front of the fireplace.

9. She has a bun in the _____. She is 6 months pregnant.

(Answers are on page 247.)

Finding Recipes Online

You don't need to buy a recipe book since there are many wonderful recipes online that are free. You can also look up recipes from television shows, such as the Food Network. Some popular websites include *epicurious.com, allrecipes.com,* and *goodhousekeeping.com.* What might you want to find on these websites?

List the ingredients for a recipe you plan to make. How many people does it serve? How many vocabulary words from this chapter did you use in the recipe?

_____

_____

_____

_____

_____

_____

(Answers will vary.)

What is left to do in the kitchen? Is Sofia going to go all out and cook more? Let's find out in the next dialogue.

DIALOGUE 3

Sofia: I am in the mood to cook some more. What do you want to eat this week? I'm going to cook for the whole week.

Juan: Can you simmer some different vegetables for me?

Sofia: Yeah, that's easy to do. I was thinking of roasting some vegetables, though, because I want to also make a pork roast.

Juan: Okay, that works for me.

Sofia: I got a new glaze that I think could be delicious drizzled over the roast and vegetables.

Juan: Oh, that sounds good. Do you want me to caramelize some onions to put in it, too?

Sofia: Sure, I love caramelized onions. They taste nice and sweet if you cook them with butter.

Juan: Okay, I'll cook them and pour them over the food.

Sofia: Just let me drain the extra liquid from the roast before you pour them on.

Juan: Do you have honey mustard or other condiments? I like to dip my veggies in condiments.

Sofia: Yes, of course I have some. I guess we are ready to cook. I think we will have enough leftovers for a few days, but not for the week. Oh well, that is still pretty good.

> **go all out:** an idiom meaning to put forth utmost effort. Example: He will go all out and make plenty of food when his family comes to visit.
>
> **simmer:** to cook something without letting it boil. Example: Once the soup is cooked, you should simmer it for fifteen minutes.
>
> **roast:** to cook in the oven. Example: I would like to roast chicken for dinner, but I am not sure I will have enough time.
>
> **drizzle:** to pour over something lightly. Example: She always likes to drizzle something on the food to make it look and taste delicious.

caramelize: to cook onions until they are soft and light brown. Example: I love to caramelize onions to put on my pork roast.

drain: to remove the liquid from something, such as a pan. Example: She should drain the fat from the pan before adding in the gravy.

condiments: things to add to food for flavor, such as ketchup and hot sauce. Example: My favorite condiment is ketchup, so I put it on all of my food.

Chapter Reflection

The following is a summary of what was covered in this chapter. What did you learn? When are you going to get to use some of this new vocabulary? How about the idioms? Go to a restaurant and use some of them with the waiter.

Vocabulary

eat out	ounce	abundance
indulge	seasoning	container
appetizer sampler	mango	creating
vegetarian	glaze	simmer
boil	coat	roast
microwave	sprinkle	drizzle
assistance	edge	caramelize
ingredients	overcook	drain
recipe	ratatouille	condiments
serving	leftover	

Idioms

know your way around the kitchen	a toast
good to the last drop	bun in the oven
hats off to the chef	nuke it
stirring the pot	if you can't take the heat,
shaken up	stay out of the kitchen
toasty	go all out

Here's an idea: Look for a recipe online! As you look for a recipe you like, notice all of the vocabulary words covered in this chapter. Then, write down the ingredients (or take a picture) and go to the grocery store to buy them. Invite a friend to help you eat what you make so that you can practice some of the idioms from this chapter.

CHAPTER 4

Eating Out

After reading this chapter, you should know more about . . .

- **Different types of restaurants in the United States**
- **Tipping for service**
- **Ordering food**
- **Using vocabulary about eating out, such as:**
  - Fast food
  - Drive-through window
  - Appetizers
  - Reservation
  - Food allergy

Who Eats Out in the United States?

Eating out is very popular in the United States. Many people like to get quick meals at inexpensive restaurants. See the following example of a conversation, or dialogue, about going out for a quick lunch. You can listen to the audio, too.

DIALOGUE 1

Juan: Would you like to meet me for lunch tomorrow? It will have to be a quick bite, because I only have 45 minutes for lunch. I also don't want to spend too much money. Where can we go?

Sofia: Well, if you only have 45 minutes and not much money, I guess it will have to be fast food.

Juan: I think it's interesting that in America, they actually have a term like fast food to mean a certain type of place to eat out.

Sofia: Yes, but some of them have healthy choices. My favorite fast food place is Wendy's. I love their salads!

Juan: Wendy's it is, then! There is one on the way to work.

Sofia: We can use the drive-through window and eat our lunch in the park.

Juan: Sounds good to me. I don't really like salads, but I do want to eat something healthy.

Sofia: You can go online and look at their menu. There are pictures of all of the food. If you click on something, it will give you the nutritional information for the food. I know that the apple pecan chicken salad I like has 570 calories and 38 grams of protein.

Juan: That's a great idea. I will take a look before we go. It sounds like you really can make healthy choices at a fast food restaurant if you take the time to research a little online before you go. My friend has a food allergy and cannot eat gluten. Does the website tell you about the ingredients in the menu choices?

Sofia: Yes, it does provide a list of the ingredients for each menu item. So many people have food allergies, and they need to know what's in their food.

Juan: I'll let him know about this. Thanks, Sofia. See you tomorrow!

quick bite: a fast meal. Example: She went to Wendy's to grab a quick bite on her way home because she was really hungry.

fast food: food, such as hamburgers, pizza, or fried chicken, prepared in the same way every time to get it ready quickly. Example: It is not a good idea to eat fast food all of the time because it can be unhealthy.

drive-through window: a type of service at fast food restaurants that lets customers buy food and drinks without leaving their cars. Example: If you go through the drive-through window, it will be faster than going inside to get your food—as long as the line is short outside.

menu: a list of the dishes served at a restaurant. Example: I hope the waiter brings out the menu soon so we can order.

nutrition: food necessary to be able to function, be healthy, and have energy. Example: Good nutrition is important for good health.

nutritional: relating to the process of providing or obtaining the food necessary to be healthy.

Example: What are the nutritional benefits of this meal?

calorie: unit of measure for the energy in food that provides fuel for our bodies. Example: If you count every calorie you eat, you can figure out if you are eating too much.

protein: plant or animal substances considered an essential food source. Example: Protein is necessary to have a balanced diet.

food allergy: a sensitivity to a certain food or food group, which can sometimes lead to death if not treated immediately. Example: I don't have any food allergies, but Juan is allergic to peanuts.

gluten: a substance that makes dough elastic or stretchy, which can make some people sick. Example: There are now gluten-free choices on some menus.

ingredient: an item in a recipe; for example, spaghetti sauce might need ingredients such as salt, garlic, oregano, onions, tomatoes, and cooking wine. Example: My favorite ingredient in most recipes is garlic.

WRITE IT DOWN

What else might you want to learn about a fast food restaurant on its website? Go to a fast food restaurant's website and tell us the nutritional information for something you might eat.

_____

_____

_____

_____

_____

_____

(Answers will vary.)

Use the following words in a sentence.

For example:
food allergy: *My friend has a food allergy, so she has to be careful what she eats at restaurants.*

gluten: _____

_____

nutritional: _____

_____

menu: _____

_____

calorie: _____

_____

protein: _____

_____

ingredient: _____

_____

(Answers will vary.)

TRUE OR FALSE

Let's see what you know about eating out in the True or False activity. Write TRUE or FALSE next to the following sentences, and later check the answer key at the end of the book for the correct answers.

_____ **1.** Eating at a fast food restaurant would not cost much money.

_____ **2.** You can get fast food at any restaurant.

_____ **3.** All restaurants have drive-through windows.

_____ **4.** You can check the Internet for nutritional information of the food in many restaurants.

_____ **5.** Gluten is good for everyone.

_____ **6.** Adding ranch dressing increases the number of calories.

_____ **7.** Protein and gluten are the same thing.

(Answers are on page 247.)

Eating Out at a Restaurant

There are many types of restaurants in the United States that are good for eating out on special occasions, such as birthdays or anniversaries. Or maybe you just want to go out for a nice meal that you don't have to cook yourself. See the following example of a dialogue about going out for dinner. You can listen to the audio, too.

DIALOGUE 2

Juan: Next Friday is my birthday, and I want to go out for a good meal. Do you want to come?

Sofia: Absolutely! Do you have a restaurant in mind? If it's a nice place, we might need to make a reservation.

Juan: Let's use the app Open Table to look for a good place. I like that you can read the reviews of the different restaurants to help you make your choice.

Sofia: Good idea. I like that they use different numbers of dollar signs to show how expensive a place is. Look, Sam's Grille has several choices. I like the list of appetizers here, too. It has four dollar signs though.

Juan: That's okay. It's my birthday, so we can splurge on a special meal.

Sofia: If you say so! Look, the reviews are almost all five stars. Let's see if we can make a reservation for next Friday.

Juan: Great, it looks like we reserved a table for 7:00 p.m. I'm even going to wear a jacket and tie because Open Table says the place is upscale.

Sofia: I'll get dressed up, too. This is going to be fun!

Juan: Dinner is on me. My parents sent a generous check for my birthday and said to go out and celebrate.

Sofia: Thank you! I will take care of the gratuity then. Did you know that in America, you should tip 20 percent of the bill for good service?

Juan: A great server deserves it! Sounds like we have a plan. I'll pick you up at 6:30 on Friday. We'll use the valet parking at the restaurant. See you next week!

reservation: having a restaurant save a table for a certain date and time. Example: He made a reservation for dinner at eight o'clock because the earlier times were already taken.

app: short for "application," an app is a program that helps a computer, phone, or tablet do a specific job, like getting the weather report or allowing someone to read books online. Example: He has an app on his phone to make reservations at restaurants.

review: a person's opinion about something, like a book, movie, or restaurant, written for others to read. Example: The reviews for that restaurant said that it was a place that everyone should experience.

expensive: something that costs a lot of money. Example: We like to go to an expensive restaurant on special occasions, such as our anniversary.

appetizers: small portions of food eaten before the main meal. Example: She likes to get appetizers to share with her friends.

splurge: to spend more than you normally do. Example: Let's splurge this weekend and go out to eat on Saturday and Sunday before we start our diet on Monday.

upscale: excellent quality, can be expensive. Example: That restaurant is upscale, and you know it because it requires men to wear a tie.

on me: an expression that means you will pay the

bill. Example: Today, lunch is on me because it is your birthday.

generous: providing more than is normally expected. Example: She is always very generous with the amount of food she puts on your plate when you eat at her house.

gratuity: a tip, or the amount of money you leave in addition to the bill for good service. Example: How much gratuity should I leave—20 percent?

valet parking: a service in which someone parks your car for you when you arrive at a restaurant and returns it to you when you are ready to leave. Example: Valet parking is nice because you don't have to worry about finding a parking space.

Vocabulary Crossword 1

Complete the crossword below using the vocabulary you just learned.

ACROSS

3. This is better than average and costs more, too.

5. When you spend more money than usual

6. You put this in a recipe.

10. A small dish you can order before the meal

11. When you give more than expected you are ____ .

12. What is a list of food dishes in a restaurant called?

DOWN

1. This makes some people sick.

2. A unit of energy in food

4. What do we call something that costs a lot of money?

7. The process of taking in and using food

8. A tip of money for a service

9. A plant or animal tissue needed in a diet

(Answers are on page 247.)

Describe the steps you would take to treat a good friend to an upscale meal for his or her birthday. Tell us what website you would use to do research, what is important to you in a restaurant, and when you plan to go.

_____

_____

_____

_____

_____

_____

(Answers will vary.)

MATCHING

Match the following words to their definitions.

A. Reservation

B. Gratuity

C. Appetizer

D. Nutrition

E. Ingredients

F. Food allergy

G. App

H. Reviews

I. Expensive

J. Splurge

K. Upscale

L. On me

M. Generous

1. _____ money given for good service at a restaurant

2. _____ a small amount of food you can order before the big meal comes

3. _____ favorable or unfavorable opinions about a meal or movie

4. _____ a reaction in some people to eating particular food, sometimes resulting in death

5. _____ giving more money or time to someone than usual

6. _____ a fancy or expensive place

7. _____ the individual items in a recipe

8. _____ when you say to someone you are treating him/her

9. _____ a way to make sure you can be seated in a restaurant at a certain time

10. _____ a program that helps a computer, phone, or tablet do a small job

11. _____ spending more money on something than you normally would

12. _____ something that costs a lot of money

13. _____ eating healthy is a good way to get this

(Answers are on page 247.)

Idioms Related to Eating Out

As you have learned, idioms are phrases that do not make sense when you translate them but are used by Americans all of the time. Therefore, it is a good idea to learn them in order to understand native English speakers more easily. There are many idioms related to food and/or eating out.

big cheese	an important person
down the hatch	swallow or drink quickly
dressed to the nines	all dressed up to look your best
eating out of your hand	being very cooperative
hit the spot	to fully satisfy and refresh, especially with food or drink
no spring chicken	not young anymore
too many cooks in the kitchen	the more people who work on one project, the worse it will turn out
bun in the oven	referring to being pregnant
worth your salt	deserving the pay or reward that you get
go cold turkey	stop doing something immediately, such as quitting smoking
cup of joe	cup of coffee
egg someone on	encourage someone to do something
pie in the sky	an idea that sounds good but is not likely to happen

STOP AND THINK

Complete each sentence by using one of the idioms related to eating out.

1. After finishing a big and delicious meal, one of the guests said, "That really hit the _____ ."

2. When the thirsty man was ready to swallow his drink, he looked up and said, "Down the _____ ."

3. In order to get a decision about what to do, we need to talk to the boss or the big _____ .

4. When she came through the door all dressed up, one her friends said, "Wow, she is dressed to the _____ ."

5. When we found such an excellent cook, the manager told the cook, "You are worth your _____ ."

Dressed to the nines

6. When the new runner who looked a lot older than the rest of the team came on the field, I heard someone say, "Well, it looks like he is no spring _____ ."

7. When her friends saw the bulge in their friend's stomach, one of them said, "Maybe she has a bun in the _____ ."

8. He should just go cold _____ and stop eating sweets to lose weight.

9. I have a cup of _____ every morning.

10. You shouldn't egg someone _____ to do something they don't want to do if it is dangerous.

11. I like his ideas, but they are pie in the _____ .

12. When the babysitter told the mom she planned to show the children some of their favorite movies, the mom said, "If you do that, you will have them eating out of your _____ ."

(Answers are on page 248.)

DIALOGUE 3

Let's hear about another night eating out with Juan and Sofia. As you listen to the following dialogue, underline the idioms that are used.

Juan: Sam's Grille was great last night, wasn't it?

Sofia: I loved it! It was really fun getting dressed to the nines, don't you think?

Juan: Well, sure, but I was thinking about the food.

Sofia: You have to admit it was fun going out to eat at such a nice place.

Juan: Yes, but it was the food preparation that stood out to me. Each dish was delicious. And, the presentation of the food was amazing! It looked as good as it tasted.

Sofia: I liked that you could see into the kitchen. No need to worry about cross-contamination there. The place was spotless.

Juan: The waiter was good, too.

Sofia: He never let our glasses get empty. He was very attentive.

Juan: So, let's start saving up for your birthday!

preparation: the way food is prepared or made. Example: The preparation required for that meal is quite complicated.

presentation: the way food is served and arranged on a plate. Example: I love going to that restaurant because the presentation of the food is fantastic, and it tastes wonderful, too.

stood out: was noticeable and distinctive. Example: That appetizer stood out from the rest because it had a creamy sauce.

cross-contamination: when you allow different types of food to touch during preparation, such as vegetables and raw meat, potentially resulting in illness when eaten. Example: It is important to avoid cross-contamination with raw meats, especially when you plan to eat the vegetables raw.

spotless: very clean. Example: She keeps her kitchen spotless at all times.

waiter: a person whose job is to serve guests at a restaurant. Example: The waiter should bring out the food soon because we have been waiting for twenty minutes already.

attentive: checking on you a lot; giving you a lot of attention. Example: A waiter that is very attentive should get a good tip.

saving up: saving money for something in the future. Example: She was saving up to go on an island vacation in the spring.

Vocabulary Crossword 2

Complete the crossword below using the vocabulary you just learned.

ACROSS

2. When something is very clean
5. Getting food ready for a meal
6. Checking on you a lot to see if you need or want anything
7. The way food is served and arranged on a plate

DOWN

1. Allowing different foods to touch when preparing them
3. The dessert ____ out as the best part of the meal.
4. A person who waits on customers in a restaurant

(Answers are on page 248.)

DINNER AND A MOVIE

One weekend, Juan and Sofia wanted to go out for pizza and a movie, but they couldn't afford to do both because they were saving up for Sofia's birthday dinner. They sat down to think. "I've got it!" they both said at the same time. Juan went online and ordered a large pepperoni and mushroom pizza from Pizza Etc. Sofia ran home to check her movie collection. She brought over a DVD they both had wanted to see when it was playing in movie theaters. She had been saving it for a time when they could watch it together. Sofia also brought some microwave popcorn. They ended up having dinner and a movie after all, at a price they could afford!

1. What was Juan and Sofia's problem in the story?

_____

_____

2. How did they solve their problem?

_____

_____

(Answers are on page 248.)

Now write your own story about Juan and Sofia going out to eat. Try to use some of the new vocabulary terms you have learned in this chapter.

_____

_____

_____

_____

_____

_____

(Answers will vary.)

Chapter Reflection

The following is a summary of what was covered in this chapter, from different types of restaurants in America, to tipping for service, to ordering food. You should go out to eat and work on asking the waiter questions about the menu. Look over this chapter before you go to remember the vocabulary and idioms you can use.

Vocabulary

quick bite	ingredient	gratuity
fast food	reservation	valet parking
drive-through window	app	preparation
menu	review	presentation
nutrition	expensive	stood out
nutritional	appetizers	cross-contamination
calorie	splurge	spotless
protein	upscale	waiter
food allergy	on me	attentive
gluten	generous	saving up

Idioms

big cheese	bun in the oven
down the hatch	worth your salt
dressed to the nines	go cold turkey
eating out of your hand	cup of joe
hit the spot	egg someone on
no spring chicken	pie in the sky
too many cooks in the kitchen	

Do you remember all of the information from this chapter? If not, go back and review to make sure you do. Practice the vocabulary and idioms in your conversations, and look for them when you are reading different materials. Better yet, go to a restaurant and try to use some of the idioms you learned while having a conversation with a friend. By practicing what you just learned at a restaurant, you can read the menu and look for some of the vocabulary you covered in this chapter.

CHAPTER 5

Banking and Money

After reading this chapter, you should know more about . . .

- **Budgeting**

- **Opening a bank account**

- **Vocabulary about banking and money, such as:**

    - Direct deposit

    - Debit card

    - Fraud

We All Need Money

Everyone needs money in order to pay the bills. It is very nice to have extra money to buy things you want but don't really need, such as a new pair of shoes or a new video game. However, financial problems can be very stressful. What are some good ways to budget your money? Let's see how Juan and Sofia budget their money in the first dialogue.

DIALOGUE 1

Sofia: I find budgeting very easy because I don't like to go shopping. When it's time to pay the bills, I still have most of my paycheck.

Juan: Well, that's not the case for me. I like to buy a new video game every time I get my paycheck. The problem is that sometimes I want to buy two or more video games, so I charge it on my credit card.

Sofia: Charging things because you don't have the money to buy them can be a bad idea if you let it get you into debt.

Juan: Yeah, I'm now in debt. I owe approximately $2,000 on one credit card and $1,000 on another credit card.

Sofia: You should think about that the next time you want to buy a video game. Maybe you can buy one only if you have the cash and it is on sale.

Juan: Yes, waiting for them to go on sale is a good idea, but I need some willpower.

Sofia: My friend has a picture of her family on her credit card to remind her that she should save money. Maybe you can get a picture of something on yours for the same reason.

Juan: I'd like to buy a house one day. Maybe I should put a picture of my dream house on the card. I should also probably go to the ATM or use the mobile app to check my account balance before buying things I don't really need.

Sofia: Then you would also avoid overdrawing your account in the future, too.

Juan: Yeah, seriously! I don't want to get a bad credit score.

Sofia: How do you get a bad credit score?

Juan: Well, the credit score depends on things like how much you owe, your credit history, and what kinds of credit you have.

Sofia: I wonder what mine is. I should check!

financial: related to money. Example: His financial situation is not good at the moment, so he doesn't have enough money to buy a car.

budget: a plan to make sure you have enough money to pay your bills. Example: It is important to stay on budget and not spend too much money.

paycheck: money you receive for working. Example: She used her entire paycheck to pay the rent when, ideally, she would have extra money after paying it.

credit card: a card provided by a bank or business, which can be used to pay for things; interest is charged to the card user if he/she does not pay the entire bill at the end of the month. Example: Having a credit card is important to help pay for things you absolutely need but cannot afford right now.

charge it: to use your credit card to pay for something. Example: She will charge it because she doesn't have any cash with her.

owe: when you have to pay back money that you borrowed or used, such as on a credit card or through a loan. Example: How much will I owe after buying the house?

debt: money you owe. Example: If you are in debt, you should try to pay it off soon.

approximately: about. Example: That will cost approximately $25.00.

cash: physical money, such as bills and coins. Example: Sherri tried to always pay for things in cash so she wouldn't get into debt.

on sale: being sold at a cheaper price than usual. Example: I am going to wait and see if that skirt goes on sale before buying it.

willpower: when you can control yourself (in this case, stop yourself from buying things you do not need). Example: It takes some people a lot of willpower to not spend too much money.

account balance: how much money you have in the bank. Example: My account balance never matches what I think I have in it.

ATM: an abbreviation for automated teller machine, a computerized machine that allows you to take money out of your account, put money into your account, and check your account balance. Example: The ATM is a very convenient way to deposit checks.

overdrawing: when you spend money that you do not have in your account. Example: You should avoid overdrawing your account because you will have to pay additional fees.

credit score: a number that shows how well you can pay your debts. Example: She has a good credit score, so she will be able to get a loan to buy that car.

WRITE IT DOWN

How do you (or might you) budget your money to make sure you have enough to pay your bills? Tell us a story about that using three or more vocabulary words you just learned.

_____

_____

_____

_____

_____

_____

(Answers will vary.)

Opening a Bank Account

There are a few different options to choose from when opening a bank account. You can get a **checking account**, from which you can easily pay your bills and write checks, or a **savings account**, which you can use to deposit and save money. A savings account also builds **interest**, which means the bank will give you a small amount of money on a regular basis just because it is holding your money. You can also have your paychecks go right  into your bank account using **direct deposit**. In addition, you could get a **safe deposit box** at the bank to put in any things you want to keep safe, such as jewelry, important documents, or other **valuables** you don't want to have in your house. The safe deposit boxes come in different sizes; the bigger they get, the more expensive they are. For a small to medium box, the **fee** is about $50 a year. You can also apply for a credit card to help you pay for things, but you need to be careful not to charge things you cannot pay for later on.

checking account: an account in which you can add money, withdraw money, or write checks using money from the account. Example: She had $500 in her checking account before she wrote that check for $399.

savings account: an account for depositing and/or keeping money without spending it regularly; this type of account also earns interest. Example: She had been putting money in her savings account for years, so she was able to save $30,000 for a new car.

interest: the money your account earns by being in the bank. Example: That bank does not have a great interest rate, which is why I went to a different bank.

direct deposit: a payment made electronically from one account to another. Example: He likes to get direct deposit instead of having to get a check in the mail.

safe deposit box: a box that you can rent from a bank to keep some of your expensive things in, such as jewelry. Example: She started keeping all of her jewelry in a safe deposit box after her house was robbed.

valuables: things that are expensive. Example: When you are out in public, you should always keep an eye on your valuables, such as your purse, cell phone, or camera.

fee: when you have to pay for a service. Example: You have to pay a fee each year if you want to have a safe deposit box.

Let's see what you know about banking in this True or False activity. Write TRUE or FALSE next to the following sentences, and later check the answer key at the end of the book for the correct answers.

_____ **1.** A bank teller is a person who helps you with your bank accounts.

_____ **2.** Most banks are open seven days a week.

_____ **3.** People can deposit checks either using an ATM or with a bank teller.

_____ **4.** The bank does not pay you very much money for keeping your money in the bank.

_____ **5.** People can talk to a banker about their financial troubles to get tips or advice.

_____ **6.** A financial advisor is a person at the bank who can help you plan your financial future.

_____ **7.** You cannot get a credit card at your bank.

_____ **8.** Everyone deposits checks in person at the bank.

_____ **9.** You can pay your bills online through your bank account.

_____ **10.** You can transfer (or switch) money from your checking account to your savings account online.

_____ **11.** Credit scores range from 300 to 850, with 850 being the best score you can get.

(Answers are on page 248.)

Idioms Related to Money

Idioms can sound funny or weird. Read over the following idioms, and share which ones you think sound odd.

time is money	time is valuable
money talks	you can get your way with money
dirt poor	when you don't have a lot of money
money to burn	having more money than is needed
throw money around	to spend your money without being careful about budgeting
in the money	when you have a lot of money; wealthy
bank on it	you can count on it
a pretty penny	it costs a lot of money
rob Peter to pay Paul	ask for money from one person to give it to another person you owe money to
cash cow	a good investment
break the bank	spend too much money

WRITE IT DOWN

Which idioms sounded funny or weird to you? Write them down and explain why.

_____

_____

_____

_____

_____

_____

(Answers will vary.)

STORY TIME

Read the following story about banking and money, and answer the questions that follow.

Juan was hoping to start saving money, so he decided to find a cash cow. He thought he could start his own online business selling old video games and other things he had around the house. However, it was not as easy as he thought. At first, he placed ads on Craigslist, but not that many people were calling him. Then he decided to put them on eBay, but since he was dirt poor, he could not pay their fees. He thought about how time was money, so he went out to find a second job on the weekends at the grocery store. However, he was not going to be able to throw money around with that small paycheck.

1. Why did Juan decide to get a job?

    A. He was bored on the weekends.

    B. He wanted to save money.

    C. He wanted to buy more video games.

2. How many ways did Juan try to make money?

    A. 1

    B. 2

    C. 3

3. Was Juan about to find a cash cow?

    A. Yes

    B. No

4. Juan thought time is money. What did he mean?

    A. He did not have time to waste.

    B. He loves money.

    C. He wanted to have a lot of time.

5. Why couldn't Juan throw money around?

    A. He wanted his friend to throw the money around.

    B. He was tired.

    C. He did not have a lot of money.

(Answers are on page 248.)

How about Sofia? Does she have any other tips about managing money? Let's find out in the next dialogue. Underline the vocabulary words and idioms you have learned as you read the dialogue.

DIALOGUE 2

Sofia: Hey, Juan, have you heard about the credit card fraud going on lately?

Juan: Do you mean how people can steal your credit card number and buy things online?

Sofia: No, I mean how some people have placed a small charge on many people's credit cards. Since the charge is very small, like only a few dollars, people don't notice it on their bill.

Juan: I guess some people must have noticed it though.

Sofia: Yeah, so it's a good idea to check your credit card statement carefully every month to make sure all of the charges on there are things you actually bought.

Juan: I usually just look over the bill quickly, but I will be more careful.

Sofia: It's especially important with your debit card, because you don't want all of your hard-earned money taken by a thief.

Juan: I will try not to use my debit card unless I am at the bank. I can use my credit card and pay that bill at the end of the month.

Sofia: That is what I started doing, because at least that way if someone tries to charge something on it, I can call and have the charge removed. If someone steals money from your bank account, I am not sure that you can get it back.

Juan: That is a good tip.

Sofia: I don't have money to burn, so I try to take care of the money I have.

Juan: I don't either. And everything seems to cost a pretty penny these days.

Sofia: You can bank on it. Ha ha ha.

(Answers are on page 248.)

> **fraud:** a scam in which people try to steal your money by pretending they are you. Example: She was found guilty of credit card fraud, so she will be going to prison for some time.
>
> **credit card statement:** the credit card bill listing purchases, payments, and interest charged by the bank issuing the card. Example: It is important to carefully look over your credit card statement each month to make sure there are no extra charges that you did not make yourself.
>
> **debit card:** a card that can be used so that the money to pay for something comes right out of your checking account. Example: Jim used his debit card to buy groceries because he never carried cash.

Write a story about an experience you had in a bank or with money, or make one up. Try to use five or more vocabulary words or idioms from this chapter.

_____

_____

_____

_____

_____

_____

(Answers will vary.)

Idiom Crossword

Complete the crossword below using the idioms you just learned.

ACROSS

3. My friend acts like she has money to ____ because she is always buying things.

4. How can he rob ____ to pay Paul? Doesn't he feel bad doing that?

5. ____ is money, so don't waste time.

6. Money ____, so if you want to get that car, tell them what you can pay for it.

7. I hope to find my ____ cow before I turn 50 years old.

9. He made a lot of money working on the weekends, so he is in the ____.

DOWN

1. Sofia is going to your party. You can ____ on it.

2. I really don't have any money. I am ____ poor.

3. She spent too much money. Did she ____ the bank?

6. If you ____ money around, you might end up with no money.

8. Those shoes cost a pretty ____. I spent a lot of money on them.

(Answers are on page 248.)

It can be fun to use idioms. Some people use them a lot more than others do. Let's see how many idioms Sofia and Juan use in the following dialogue.

DIALOGUE 3

Juan: I know that a house costs a pretty penny, but I am going to save enough money so that I can buy one.

Sofia: Hopefully you will find a cash cow. Wouldn't that be nice?

Juan: Yes, because even though I don't plan to throw money around, it would be nice to make money quickly.

Sofia: Well, as we know, money talks. We have to make money to spend money.

Juan: I am working on it. The weekend job is actually pretty interesting, and I feel good because I am no longer dirt poor.

Sofia: I bet you don't have to rob Peter to pay Paul anymore.

Juan: No, I am starting to get out of my debt. It will be a while before I have money to burn, but it just feels good to be paying it off.

Sofia: I guess I'd better go to work now. Time is money.

How many idioms did they use? _____

(Answer is on page 248.)

Chapter Reflection

The following is a summary of what was covered in this chapter, which includes information about budgeting and opening a bank account, and vocabulary about banking and money. Make sure to follow the tips provided to help you with your money.

Vocabulary

financial	on sale	direct deposit
budget	willpower	safe deposit box
paycheck	account balance	valuables
credit card	ATM	fee
charge it	overdrawing	fraud
owe	credit score	credit card statement
debt	checking account	debit card
approximately	savings account	
cash	interest	

Idioms

time is money	bank on it
money talks	a pretty penny
dirt poor	rob Peter to pay Paul
money to burn	cash cow
throw money around	break the bank
in the money	

Do you remember all of the information from this chapter? If not, go back and review it to make sure you do. Practice the vocabulary and idioms in your conversations, and look for them when you are reading different materials. It would be helpful if you could go to a bank and talk to a financial planner or bank teller to get advice about credit cards and financial planning. If you make an appointment at your local bank, they can help you open an account to best organize your money. Make an appointment today just to see what advice they might have for you.

CHAPTER 6

Finding a Place to Live

After reading this chapter, you should know more about . . .

- **The benefits of renting versus buying**

- **Figuring out the distance to public transportation or work**

- **Using vocabulary related to this, such as the following:**

    - Traffic

    - Congested

    - Commute

    - Row house/Townhouse

The Benefits of Renting Versus Buying

What should you do: rent or buy a property? Do you want to stay in the area for several years? Or do you want to stay in the area for only a little while? These are important questions to ask yourself before considering renting or buying. If you want to stay in the area for several years and you have some money saved for a **down payment**, you might want to buy a house. If you buy a house, you can consider it an **investment** that can hopefully help you make money when you sell it several years later. Let's see what Juan and Sofia thought about finding a place to live close to their work.

DIALOGUE 1

Sofia: I'd like to stay in one area for a while, but since I am new to this area, I'm not sure how much I am going to like it.

Juan: I know what you mean. You might want to see how much **traffic** there is or how **congested** the area is to see if you like it.

Sofia: Yeah, and I don't want the **commute** to be too long, either. I also want to try going to work different ways to see which way gets me there the fastest.

Juan: If you live close to **public transportation**, that would make the commute easier.

Sofia: I might want to buy a car later on.

Juan: A car is definitely nice to have, but you might want to go to work using public transportation anyway depending on where you are going.

Sofia: I guess it would be less **stressful** to sit back and not worry about traffic if I have a long commute.

Juan: Yes, and you might be able to find a cheaper place to live farther away from where you work.

Sofia: I had not thought of that. That's a good point. It might be worth the longer commute.

down payment: part of the full price that you pay upfront when first buying a house to help your monthly payments be lower. Example: She is lucky because her parents gave her the down payment for her house.

investment: putting your money toward something, such as a house, in an effort to make money in the future. Example: You should be careful about an investment that is risky because you can easily lose your money.

traffic: when there are many vehicles (cars, buses, or trucks) on the road. Example: There is always a lot of traffic on my way to work.

congested: having many vehicles on the road, making the ride slow. Example: Cities tend to be congested areas, which is why it is helpful to take the bus so that you don't have to drive.

commute: going to your destination, such as going from home to work. Example: Her commute is one hour to and from work every day.

public transportation: using a bus, subway, or other way to get to work that is not driving your own car. Example: If you use public transportation, you don't have to worry about finding a parking spot.

stressful: something that makes you worry or causes tension. Example: It can be stressful driving to work when there is traffic and you need to get there on time.

WRITE IT DOWN

What is more important to you? Circle A or B.

A. Living close to work with a shorter commute, but paying more money for your house

B. Living farther from work with a longer commute, but paying less money for your house

Tell us why and explain what you prefer.

_____

_____

_____

_____

_____

_____

(Answers will vary.)

Renting

If you decide to rent because you are not sure how long you will be in the area or do not have any money for a down payment, there are some helpful websites for you, such as *apartmentfinder.com, apartment.com, rent.com,* and *zillow.com.*

WRITE IT DOWN

Write down a few sentences describing what you are looking for in a home, such as the number of rooms you want, if you prefer carpet or wood flooring, if you want a yard, etc.

For example:
I would like to find a home that has two bedrooms and two bathrooms.

_____

_____

_____

_____

_____

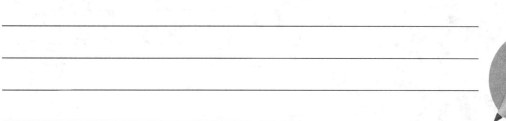

(Answers will vary.)

Another place to look for a rental home is your local newspaper. You can locate that online or at any grocery store. You will find brief listings for rental properties, but it can be a quick way to find a place to live. Let's see how Sofia and Juan looked for a rental home in this next dialogue.

DIALOGUE 2

Juan: Hey Sofia, have you found a place to live yet?

Sofia: No, I'm not sure where to move just yet. I've been looking online, but everything seems so expensive here in the city.

Juan: Well, you can always find something a little farther away from work that is cheaper, and it might be bigger or nicer.

Sofia: I might have to do that. I really wanted to live very close to work, but the only places I have found close by are very small. I found an efficiency, or studio apartment, that I could afford.

Juan: I know you wanted a one-bedroom apartment, so a studio apartment would be kind of small.

Sofia: I want to have enough space for all of my things. It would be very tight to have my living room furniture, bedroom furniture, and desk all in one room.

Juan: It could work, but it would be tight. If you look farther away, you might even be able to live in a townhouse or row house.

Sofia: I did look into that, and you're correct. For the same price that I can get a studio apartment close to work, I can get a townhouse if I commute. Or, if I wanted to stay in an apartment so that I don't have to worry about cutting the grass, I can get a one-bedroom easily.

Juan: It sounds like you are going to commute.

listings: a grouping of rental homes that are described one after the other. Example: There are several new listings this weekend, so hopefully you can find one that you like.

efficiency or studio apartment: a home that has one room or space for everything, plus a bathroom. Example: She is living by herself in an efficiency or studio apartment.

afford: to be able to pay for something. Example: She can afford to pay for the studio apartment on her own.

townhouse or row house: a home that is connected to another home by a shared wall (or walls); usually you only have neighbors on each side of you, not above or below you. Example: They moved to a townhouse, or row house, when they had children.

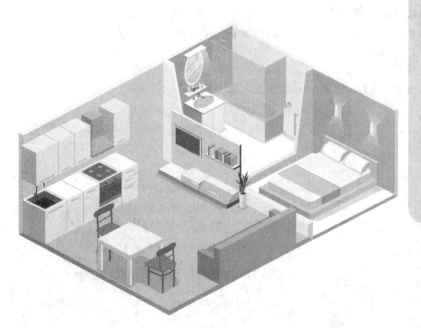

MATCHING

Let's see how much vocabulary you remember from this chapter so far. Match the following words to their definitions.

A. Down payment
B. Townhouse or row house
C. Public transportation
D. Commute
E. Efficiency or studio apartment
F. Stressful
G. Traffic
H. Afford
I. Congested
J. Investment

1. _____ a home that is connected to another home by a wall (or walls); usually you only have neighbors on each side of you, not above or below you

2. _____ an apartment that has one room or space for everything, plus a bathroom

3. _____ putting your money toward something, such as a house, in an effort to make money

4. _____ going to your destination, such as going from home to work

5. _____ part of the full price you pay upfront when buying a house to help your monthly payments be lower

6. _____ using a bus, subway, or other way to get to work that is not in your car

7. _____ something that makes you worry or causes tension

8. _____ when there are many cars, buses, or trucks on the road

9. _____ having many cars, buses, or trucks on the road, making the ride slow

10. _____ to be able to pay for something

(Answers are on page 248.)

Use the following words in a sentence:

down payment:

_____

townhouse or row house:

_____

public transportation:

_____

commute:

_____

efficiency or studio apartment:

_____

stressful:

_____

traffic:

_____

afford:

_____

congested:

_____

investment:

_____

(Answers will vary.)

Buying a House

If you have decided to stay in a location for several years, buying a house might be a good choice. You should look carefully into potential neighborhoods to make sure they have what you want. For example, do you want a good school for your child? Do you want a mall close by? Do you want theaters and other entertainment that is easy to get to? How about the level of crime? When buying a home, it is especially important to make sure your new neighborhood has what you are looking for, since you will be there a long time.

Vocabulary Crossword

Complete the crossword below using the vocabulary you just learned.

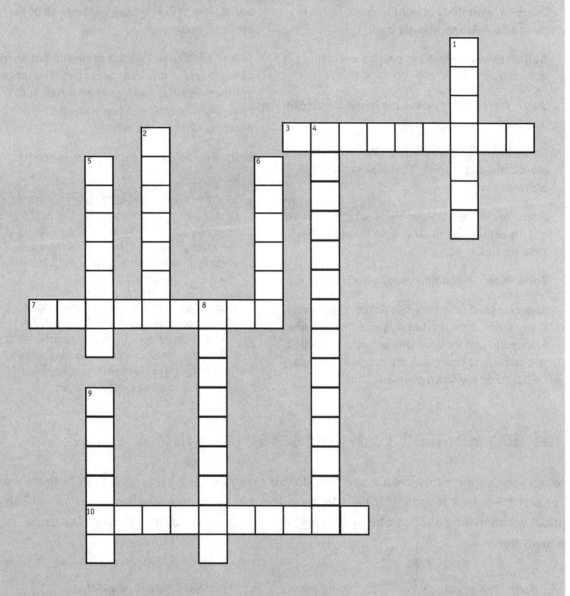

ACROSS

3. Getting to work on time can be ____.

7. I feel like it takes a very long time to get to work when traffic is ____.

10. Buying a house is considered an ____.

DOWN

1. When there are many cars on the road it means there is ____.

2. My ____ will take me about 45 minutes.

4. I plan to go on a bus or public ____.

5. He had saved $20,000 as a down ____ to buy the house.

6. I can pay for that because I have enough money. I can ____ it.

8. I like having my neighbors close by but not on top of me. I should get a ____.

9. I cannot fit into a small ____ apartment.

(Answers are on page 248.)

Let's see what Sofia and Juan think about buying a home.

Juan: I'm glad that I bought a house, because I have enjoyed making it my own.

Sofia: I like how you have painted everything in light colors.

Juan: Yes, I think it makes the house look clean and bright.

Sofia: I also like that you live close to grocery stores and pharmacies. That makes running errands easy.

Juan: Yes, it does, and on the weekend I want to get my errands done quickly so that I can have time for fun.

Sofia: How did you find your house?

Juan: I looked online on *zillow.com*. There are many other websites, but this was the first one I looked at and thought was helpful. It included the prices and how much my mortgage would be based on my down payment.

Sofia: I heard Zillow does not have all of the listings, though.

Juan: That's true. I used it at first to get an idea of the prices in different areas but then looked at other websites, such as *realtor.com*, too. You really have to look at a few websites before deciding what house to buy.

Sofia: Buying a house is a big investment!

> **errands:** going to places to get things done or purchased, such as going to the post office or grocery store. Example: It seems like all of the errands have to get done on the weekend because there is not enough time during the week to do them.
>
> **mortgage:** the amount you owe a bank for a house you purchased using a loan from that bank, paid back in monthly installments over many years. Example: You have to pay the mortgage every month on time if you don't want to pay an additional fee.

Idioms Related to Homes and Buying a Home

Idioms are expressions people use that do not make sense when you translate them word for word. For that reason, it is best to learn them in order to understand native English speakers more easily. It can be interesting and fun to learn idioms, such as the ones shown below.

going the distance	doing something until it is successfully completed
keep someone at a distance	to keep a respectful or cautious distance from someone
home is where the heart is	you feel best when you are at home
a bird in the hand is worth two in the bush	having something for sure, such as a job or a house, is better than having two things that are not for sure
money makes the world go round	you need money to function in the world
it's all about the Benjamins	everything is about money, such as how much money is needed or how much money can be saved (a *Benjamin* is a $100 bill, so called because the picture on it is of Benjamin Franklin).

Fill in the blanks using the idioms you just learned.

1. He tries not to see his cousin when he visits town. He tries to _____.

2. In order to buy or rent a house, you need to have money. It's _____.

3. He accepted the job instead of waiting to see if he had other job offers because
_____.

4. It is so much easier to buy a house if you have money saved. That is because
_____.

5. Sofia loves being at home because _____.

6. She is going to keep trying, even if it takes her a month to find the perfect place to live.
She is _____.

(Answers are on page 248.)

Idiom and Vocabulary Crossword

Complete the crossword below using the idioms and vocabulary you just learned.

ACROSS

2. Is the ____ or travel time to work okay with you?

3. Keep those at a ____ if you don't like them.

6. It is all about the ____ or it is all about the money.

7. I need to get my ____ done on the weekend to make sure I have enough food for the week.

8. A bird in the hand is worth ____ in the bush. You should consider taking that job.

10. Can you ____ that home? Do you have enough money?

DOWN

1. How much will the ____ payment be every month?

4. Is it very ____ in that area? Is there a lot of traffic?

5. He is ____ the distance to get that house. He really wants that house.

9. Money makes the ____ go round. Without money it is very hard to live.

(Answers are on page 248.)

How might you use some of those idioms? Write a sentence for each one.

going the distance

_____

keep someone at a distance

_____

home is where the heart is

_____

a bird in the hand is worth two in the bush

_____

money makes the world go round

_____

it's all about the Benjamins

_____

(Answers will vary.)

Getting to Work

Once you have a place to live, you can ease stress by looking into all of the different ways to get to work in order to find the best way. Google Maps can be very helpful for getting directions via your computer or your smartphone. You might want to plug in your phone while using your GPS, though, since that seems to quickly use up the battery. The OK Google app is wonderful. You just say "Okay Google, take me to _____ ," and it gives you directions. That app also tells you how long it will take to get to your destination in a car or bus, or by walking. It also tells you where there is a lot of traffic and gives you the fastest way to get to where you need to go. You can ask OK Google any question; it does not have to be about directions. It is a fun

app to try. If you say "Thank you" to it, it says "You're welcome." How do Sofia and Juan use OK Google? Read the following dialogue to find out.

Juan: Did you find out the best way to commute to work, Sofia?

Sofia: Yes, I learned about the OK Google app and simply asked it.

Juan: Did you have trouble with that app?

Sofia: At first I did because you have to speak a little bit slowly and clearly.

Juan: I haven't tried it, but I heard it's good. It's supposed to tell you the way with less traffic. What else can you ask OK Google?

Sofia: You can ask it anything. You can ask it questions about movie stars or can even ask it to play certain songs or videos for you.

Juan: Wow! That's very cool. I will have to get that app.

Sofia: I recommend it. I've been using it for about a year and I think it is great.

Chapter Reflection

The following is a summary of what was covered in this chapter, from renting versus buying a home, to how to figure out the distance to places, such as from home to work. Use the OK Google app today and play with it to see the distance to places around you. Then, try going somewhere nearby, using it for directions.

Vocabulary

down payment	public transportation	afford
investment	stressful	townhouse or row house
traffic	listings	errands
congested	efficiency or studio apartment	mortgage
commute		

Idioms

going the distance	a bird in the hand is worth two in the bush
keep someone at a distance	money makes the world go round
home is where the heart is	it's all about the Benjamins

Do you remember all of the information we covered in this chapter? If not, go back and review it to make sure you do. Practice the vocabulary and idioms in your conversations, and look for them when you are reading different materials. Have fun looking into different neighborhoods using some of the ideas from this chapter to see if you can find the perfect place for you, whether you rent, buy, live close to work, or have a longer commute.

CHAPTER 7

Your Home

After reading this chapter, you should know more about . . .

- **Living in a rental or your own home**
- **How to take care of the inside of a home**
- **Using household appliances and electronics**
- **Maintaining the outside of the house**
- **Vocabulary related to this chapter, such as the following:**
  - Landlord
  - Siding
  - Resident

Living in a Rental or Your Own Home

If you rent an apartment or a house, it can be easier than owning in many ways. If you rent, the **utilities** might be included in your rent, you would work with the **landlord** if you had any problems with things like plumbing, and you would not have to worry about paying for regular repairs. However, you would want to know what the **lease** says before signing it to make sure you know exactly what you are responsible for. For example, the lease might say you have to take care of certain repairs.

Or, if you wanted certain things, such as having a dog live in the residence or being able to leave in less than a year, you should make sure it is covered in the lease—that way you can have a pleasant experience in your new place.

If you buy a home, you have more **flexibility** in doing things the way you want to do them. You could have three dogs, and there would be no landlord to tell you otherwise. Yet, you would have to worry about all of the repairs yourself and would pay for all of the utilities out of your own pocket. **Nevertheless**, if you are staying in the area for many years, it might be worth the investment.

TRUE OR FALSE

Answer the following true or false statements based on what you just read.

_____ 1. If you want to have the most flexibility in being able to have pets, you should rent an apartment.

_____ 2. The utilities are always included as part of the rent.

_____ 3. A landlord is very helpful to a homeowner.

_____ 4. "In spite of" and "nevertheless" mean the same thing.

_____ 5. You should quickly sign your lease.

(Answers are on page 248.)

utilities: the bills you have to pay for the house, such as the electric and water bills. Example: He did not have enough money to pay for the utilities after he made the bathroom repair.

landlord or superintendent: the person who owns the apartment or house and rents it out, or someone who is hired by the owner to deal with the property. Example: The landlord for that house is very strict about having people pay the rent on the first of the month.

lease: a contract that says how long a property is being rented out to the renter, for what price, and under which conditions. Example: Her lease was for only six months.

flexibility: being able to adapt to things easily. Example: She really liked having the flexibility to paint her new house any color she wanted because she could not do that when she rented.

nevertheless: even though, or in spite of. Example: She wanted to eat at 6 p.m.; nevertheless, she ate at 8 p.m. because she was waiting for her friends to get out of work and join her.

Taking Care of a House or Apartment

You may live in an apartment or a house. You may be renting, or you may be the owner. In any case, the **resident** should know how to maintain the inside of a house and properly use and maintain appliances. If you are a homeowner, the level of knowledge required is greater. Maintaining the outside, or exterior, of the house as well as the **grounds** adds to your responsibilities.

The place where you live may be older and therefore will require extra **maintenance** and care. On the other hand, you may be living in a **contemporary** house with modern appliances and **technology**. In this chapter, we will take a closer look at the things a resident should know and be able to do to take care of the place where he or she lives.

> **DIALOGUE 1**

Let's see what Bob and Tracey have to say about their homes in the next dialogue.

Tracey: I have some great news! With the help of my parents, I was able to buy the little place near my college! Now I can be close to school and have a place of my own, and the price was low enough that I won't be **house poor**.

Bob: That's great news. Congratulations! I have some great news, too. My grandfather decided to move in with my parents and gave me his house.

Tracey: Wow! That's great. I've never seen his house. What is it like?

Bob: Well, it's a small house that was built about fifty years ago. I was afraid it might be a **royal pain** to fix up, but it is in pretty good shape. It has two bedrooms and a bathroom on the second floor, and a living room, dining room, and kitchen on the first floor. It also has a nice front yard, and the backyard has a small deck.

Tracey: That sounds like just the right size for you. It sounds like you won't be **biting off more than you can chew**. I can't wait to see it, and I really want you to come over and **check out** my place! When I did a **walk-through** of my new place, the former owner gave me a quick tour and showed me where the **HVAC** unit, the **thermostat**, and the **circuit breaker** box were and went over some of the appliances, like the washer and dryer. I hope I remember everything she said. She also gave me a big folder with quite a few operating manuals for all the appliances. I haven't really looked at any of them yet.

Bob: I have an idea. Let's make a list of things we think we need to know about our places. Then, when I come over to your place, we can try to figure it out together.

Tracey: That sounds like a great idea. I'll call you in a couple of days.

resident: a person living in a house or apartment. Example: He is a resident of that apartment building.

grounds: the land that surrounds a building. Example: He walked around the grounds to see how the plants were doing.

maintenance: actions to keep machines and other objects operating properly. Example: The maintenance required for the new heating system was minimal.

contemporary: belonging or occurring in the present. Example: He wanted a more contemporary look when he bought new furniture.

technology: techniques, skills, methods, and devices used to produce something or perform a task. Example: I had to learn about the technology available on my self-cleaning oven.

house poor: an idiom that means spending so much on a house that little money is left for other things. Example: He can't go to the movies very much because he is house poor.

royal pain (or headache): an idiom that means someone or something that is difficult to work with. Example: Sadly, he bought a house that has been a royal pain.

biting off more than you can chew: an idiom that means when you have taken on more work or responsibilities than you can handle. Example: You are working two jobs and going to school, so I think you are biting off more than you can chew.

check out: an idiom that means to look at or notice. Example: Come and check out my new car.

walk-through: an idiom that refers to the final inspection of a house or apartment before buying it. Example: I want my friend to join me on the walk-through so I don't miss something important that may need repair.

HVAC: an acronym for **h**eating, **v**entilation, and **a**ir **c**onditioning. Example: I don't know if my HVAC unit runs on electricity or gas.

thermostat: an electronic device, usually mounted on a wall, that controls the heat and air conditioning. Example: I got a new thermostat that can adjust the temperature for different times of the day.

circuit breaker: an electrical device that replaced fuses as a way to protect electrical circuits; circuit breakers can be reset rather than replaced like fuses. Example: The electrician added a new circuit breaker for my hot water heater.

WRITE IT DOWN

If you had to choose what type of place to live in, would you go with a house or an apartment? Explain your choice giving two or more reasons.

_____

_____

_____

_____

_____

_____

(Answers will vary.)

Maintaining the Interior of a House

Taking care of the interior of a house typically involves repairs, maintenance, and, at times, **upgrades** or improvements. The repairs, maintenance, and upgrades can be for basic **structural** components, such as ceilings, floors, walls, and windows, as well as for appliances. Most homes have washers, dryers, hot water heaters, microwaves, dishwashers, stoves, and refrigerators, and HVAC units or furnaces.

Repairs are often necessary when something has been improperly maintained, has outlived its expected life, or has a broken part. It is helpful to know the age and condition of all appliances, including the HVAC unit or furnace. Hot water heaters, for example, are often expected to last about ten years. If you are purchasing a home or an apartment, the time to find out the condition and age of these appliances is before the purchase. If you own your residence and need repairs, be sure to check whether there are **warranties** on the items. You will also want to hire **reliable** companies. You can identify reliable companies by asking friends and neighbors for recommendations as well as by accessing websites that list approved or reliable **contractors**, such as *homeadvisor.com* or *angieslist.com*.

Maintaining your appliances begins with being aware of how they work. Reading the manual that came with the equipment is very important. If you move into a house or an apartment that doesn't have the manuals, they are usually available online from the manufacturer or other sources, sometimes for a fee. What can be the most fun is upgrading or improving something in your house. For example, if you renovate your kitchen or bathroom, you can make it just how you want it. It will really make the house feel like it is your own. Improvements can also increase the value of your home.

DIALOGUE 2

Let's see what happened when Tracey shared her list with Bob.

Tracey: Well, I finally looked through all of the manuals and walked around the apartment and came up with a list to talk to you about.

Bob: I have been working on my list, but I'm anxious to see what you came up with.

Tracey: The first thing I did was make a list of all my appliances. Then, next to each appliance, I checked off whether I had the manual and whether I read it. Then, I tried to find out how old it was.

Bob: It seems like you were really on top of this. Were you able to find out how old the appliances were?

Tracey: Not at first. Then I learned that if you can locate the serial number and model number on the appliance, you can do an Internet search. I found all of them that way.

Bob: So, what does all of that information tell you?

Tracey: Well, my oldest appliance is my hot water heater. It is eleven years old. Do you think I should replace it?

Bob: That's a tough question. I heard they are expected to last about ten years. If it should leak, it could cause quite a mess to you and the apartments below you.

Tracey: I think you're right. It looks like I'll be looking for a replacement. I hope it won't cost an arm and a leg.

Bob: I think that is prudent. It looks like you are well on your way to putting your house in order.

Tracey: Pretty much, thanks to your help. Now what about your place and your list?

Bob: I think I'll be done by Friday. Mine is taking a little longer because I have outside stuff to think about, and I don't want to cut corners. How about coming over on Saturday?

Tracey: Sounds great; see you then!

upgrade: improvement on the quality and/or features of an item or service. Example: Getting a new thermostat was a simple upgrade.

structural: having to do with the basic parts (i.e., frame, walls, roof) of a building or other construction. Example: They found surprisingly little structural damage to the house after the hurricane.

warranties: written statements from a company that guarantee a product or parts of a product for a period of time. Example: Unfortunately, the warranty for my clothes dryer ran out last month.

reliable: a person or thing that performs or works consistently and as promised. Example: My father gave me the name of a reliable painter.

contractors: people who are hired to perform specific work, such as construction or repair work on houses or buildings. Example: The contractor will come next week to install the new hot water heater.

on top of it: an idiom that means you know what needs to be done and will take care of it. Example: She got her work done ahead of time because she stayed on top of it.

serial number: a number on an item to help identify it. Example: I found the serial number on a metal plate inside the refrigerator door.

model number: a number located on an item that indicates a particular model or version of an item. Example: The repairman said having the stove's model number would help him get the right parts to fix it.

cost an arm and a leg: an idiom that means something is very expensive. Example: The houses in that area cost an arm and a leg.

prudent: being wise and acting sensibly and cautiously. Example: Replacing important appliances before they fail is prudent.

put your house in order: an idiom that means to arrange your affairs or solve your problems. Example: Before going on vacation, you should put your house in order so nothing falls through the cracks while you are gone.

cut corners: an idiom that means taking shortcuts while performing a task that can result in poor work or poor quality. Example: Her house had many problems because the previous owners always cut corners.

MATCHING

Match the following words to their definitions using the vocabulary you just learned.

A. Upgrade
B. Structural
C. Warranty
D. Reliable
E. Contractor
F. Serial number
G. Model number
H. Prudent

1. _____ a limited guarantee that a product will not break

2. _____ the number on an item that is specific to only that item

3. _____ wise; not taking chances

4. _____ the number on an item indicating its particular version of that item

5. _____ an improvement to a product or service

6. _____ relating to the basic parts of something that has been constructed

7. _____ a person or thing that performs or works consistently

8. _____ a person who is hired to do specific work

(Answers are on page 248.)

Maintaining the Exterior of a House

If you are a homeowner, in addition to taking care of the inside of a house, there are a number of areas on the outside of a house that require your attention. These areas include the exterior of the house itself as well as the driveway, sidewalks, grounds, and safety lighting. Usually, the first step in maintaining the exterior is to make a thorough inspection of all the areas just mentioned. Starting with the house itself, look at the siding, windows, doors, and roof. You may also want to inspect any outbuildings, such as a garage or shed. Your inspection should not turn up signs of rot, wear, or damage.

The next areas to look at are the grounds, which include the driveway, fences, lawn, and landscaping. You want to look for cracks or settling in the driveway or sidewalks, damage or loose parts on a fence, bare patches of grass, or plants that need trimming or fertilizing. It is a good idea to keep a list of what you find. You can then figure out what should be fixed first.

siding: the material put on the sides of buildings, such as wood, metal, and vinyl, to protect and improve the appearance. Example: I think I will have to replace my vinyl siding because the color has faded.

landscaping: trees, plants, flowers, and shrubs around a home or building. Example: The new home needed all new landscaping because the land was just rocks and soil.

fertilizing: adding chemicals to plants and soil to improve growth. Example: I read that my roses need a fertilizer with nitrogen.

STORY TIME

TRACEY VISITS BOB IN HIS NEW HOUSE

On Saturday, Tracey saw Bob's new house. She surprised him with a housewarming gift. He wasn't expecting the book How to Take Care of Your Home. He said it was just the thing he needed, particularly since it covered both the interior and exterior of houses. He went on to tell her that he did the same careful inspection she had done but had concentrated on the outside of the house. Bob told her he had learned a lot about the things that the outside of the house needed. He found that the vinyl siding was in good shape but had a lot of stains and green stuff on the walls. He also found that the wood fence posts were loose. He found that some of the boards on his small deck were warped and soft and would need to be replaced. Lastly, he noticed a lot of bare spots in the grass, both in front and in back. He told Tracey that he guessed that his grandfather had not been able to keep up with the house repairs. Tracey asked him what his plan was going to be. Bob said he would make a list of projects, try to estimate the costs, and decide which things he would do first. He told her the book she got him would be very helpful.

1. A housewarming gift is a
    A. heater.
    B. check to use for the heating bill.
    C. present given to someone who has a new house.
    D. gift from a neighbor.

2. Why was the outside in need of several repairs?
    A. The house was very old.
    B. It had been a very cold winter.
    C. A repair company had done a poor job.
    D. The grandfather had not been able to keep up with all the work.

3. The first thing Bob will do to get the outside fixed is to
    A. make a list of needed repairs.
    B. start repairing the deck.
    C. begin work on the fencing.
    D. talk to his grandfather.

4. Which of the following does not seem to be a problem?
    A. The siding
    B. The roof
    C. The grass
    D. The fence

(Answers are on page 248.)

STOP AND THINK

Fill in the blanks with the most appropriate vocabulary you learned in this chapter.

1. I heard that microwaves are very reliable and therefore require little _____ .

2. I'm cold, so can you please adjust the _____ ?

3. That book on _____ helped me with my new garden.

4. I can't believe how much new _____ is in today's kitchen appliances.

5. With all the weeds I saw, I felt the _____ had been neglected.

6. They say fall is a good time for _____ the garden.

7. My _____ unit keeps me very cool in the summer.

8. My mother likes an older style of furniture, but I like a more _____ look.

9. Do you prefer wood or vinyl _____ on your house?

10. Did you know she is a _____ in your apartment building?

11. I found that the _____ really helped me take a close look at the apartment.

12. If your lights go out, you may need to reset the _____ breaker.

(Answers are on page 248.)

Idioms Related to Houses

Circle the idioms you were not familiar with before reading them in this chapter.

walk-through	an inspection of a house before purchasing or renting
check out	look at closely; notice
on top of it	knowing what needs to be done and taking care of it
put your house in order	organize your affairs and solve your problems
royal pain (or headache)	someone or something that is difficult to work with
house poor	spending so much on a house that little money is left for other things
housewarming gift	a gift given to someone who has just moved into a new home
cost an arm and a leg	when something is very expensive
bite off more than you can chew	when you have taken on more work or responsibilities than you can handle
cut corners	to take shortcuts while performing a job that can result in poor work or poor quality

Chapter Reflection

The following is a summary of what was covered in this chapter about getting your own home, including information relating to both the inside and outside of a house.

Vocabulary

utilities	thermostat	
landlord or superintendent	circuit breaker	
lease	upgrades	
flexibility	structural	
nevertheless	warranties	
resident	reliable	
grounds	contractors	
maintenance	serial number	landscaping
contemporary	model number	fertilizing
technology	prudent	
HVAC	siding	

Idioms

house poor	on top of it
royal pain	cost an arm and a leg
bite off more than you can chew	put your house in order
check out	cut corners
walk-through	housewarming gift

Do you remember all of the information covered in this chapter? If not, go back and make sure you do. Practice the vocabulary and idioms in your conversations, and look for them when reading different materials. Having a place of your own, whether you are renting or owning, brings a lot of pleasure and independence, but also a lot of responsibility. Carefully look around your home and make a list of things you may need to fix. Do some research online to find out how you might start working on them today.

Finding Work

After reading this chapter, you should know more about . . .

- **Searching for a job**
- **Refining your résumé**
- **Going to an interview**
- **Using work-related vocabulary, such as the following:**

    - Goals
    - Prioritize
    - Classifieds
    - Idioms like *do the dirty work* and *works for me*

Finding a Job

Where should you search for a job? There are many places to look for work. It might be good to begin by simply asking people you know about job opportunities. Talk to more people, meet new people, and attend events related to your work; that way you can hear firsthand what people in your field suggest. You can also connect with people in your field of work online through LinkedIn, or you can look for job boards online related to your field and post your résumé there. Tip: If you update your résumé often on a job board, it will stay toward the top of the list of résumés.

DIALOGUE 1

Let's see what Juan and Sofia did to update their résumés.

Juan: Hey, Sofia, can you look at my résumé? I would love it if you could edit it for me. I want to make sure it doesn't have any mistakes. I want to see if there's a better job out there for me.

Sofia: I'd be happy to look at yours if you will look at mine! I have been thinking of looking for a new job, too.

Juan: Sure, I can do that, but I am not that good at proofreading.

Sofia: Okay, well, you can look to see if it is clear.

Juan: I can help you with that.

Sofia: Did you use an interesting format?

Juan: What do you mean?

Sofia: Well, there are some cool-looking ways to make your résumé stand out from the rest. For example, there are some free résumé templates on the Creative Bloq website *creativebloq.com.*

Juan: I'll have to look into that idea. It would be good to stand out.

Sofia: You could also make a video of yourself, post it on YouTube, and provide the link on your résumé to stand out even more.

opportunities: possibilities or options. Example: He has many job opportunities in Chicago.

firsthand: direct or personal observation or experience. Example: She can tell you about him firsthand because she used to work with him.

LinkedIn: a website where you can find jobs of interest and can post your résumé. Example: Many people use LinkedIn to network with people in similar fields or jobs.

résumé: a summary of your work history that you provide to possible employers. Example: A résumé should have no errors or typos on it and should be easy to understand.

edit: to correct writing. Example: You will need to edit your résumé to make sure it is perfect before sending it out to employers.

proofreading: reading something while looking for errors, such as in spelling, punctuation, grammar, and formatting. Example: She is proofreading her cover letter one more time to make sure it is perfect.

format: the layout or organization on a page. Example: The format of your résumé should be simple and clear.

stand out: an idiom meaning to look different than the rest. Example: To make a résumé stand out from the rest, you could add in video links or format it a little differently.

template: an outline or model used to help with writing. Example: There are many templates online that can help you format your résumé.

WRITE IT DOWN

Have you ever thought about making your résumé stand out from the rest? Look at different résumé templates online and tell us what you like and don't like, and how you might want to update your own résumé.

_____

_____

_____

_____

_____

_____

(Answers will vary.)

STOP AND THINK 1

Use the vocabulary you just learned to fill in the following blanks.

1. Juan was working on fixing his _____ .

2. To find job _____ , you can look online or find meetings related to your field.

3. The _____ of your résumé should help you to stand out.

4. There are some neat-looking résumé _____ on the Creative Bloq website.

5. You should definitely proofread and _____ your résumé before giving it to a possible employer.

6. It is a good idea to meet with people _____ to find out about job opportunities.

(Answers are on page 249.)

DIALOGUE 2

Once you have your résumé ready to go, where do you start your job search? There are many places to search these days. Let's see where Sofia and Juan are going to look.

Juan: I thought I might look in the newspaper's classifieds to find a job.

Sofia: Oh, really? That's pretty old school.

Juan: I figured it would be a good place to start. It might give me ideas of other places to look, too.

Sofia: That's true. I was going to suggest you look at websites of companies or organizations in the area to see if they have any job postings.

Juan: I thought about that, too. How about getting a headhunter or recruiter?

Sofia: I don't know. Have you used one before?

Juan: No, that's why I was asking you.

Sofia: All I know is that a headhunter or recruiter is a person that can help you find jobs, but they charge a big fee.

Juan: I guess I won't be using a headhunter then.

Sofia: I won't be using one either. I think we can find what we are looking for by making connections with people face-to-face or online. I already started looking at organizations related to my field to see if they have any events I can attend.

Juan: I started looking at websites, like LinkedIn, Monster, and Indeed.

Sofia: I never heard of Indeed. Is it like Monster?

Juan: Yeah, it's very similar. We should prioritize what we want and then look for a job on those websites.

classifieds: a section in the newspaper that lists things for sale, job advertisements, services, announcements, and events. Example: She found her job in the classifieds.

old school: an idiom meaning an old-fashioned way of doing something. Example: Her boss is old school and prefers to meet people in person rather than on Skype.

headhunter: a person who can help people who are looking for jobs and also help employers who are seeking people for certain jobs. Example: Many people were recruited by a headhunter for that position.

recruiter: a person who looks for people needed in certain jobs; they can be similar to a headhunter. Example: The recruiter did an excellent job finding people who were qualified for the job.

fee: a price that needs to be paid. Example: Recruiters always charge a fee for their services.

face-to-face: in direct contact with. Example: After the Skype interviews, some people were invited to the next step, which was the face-to-face interviews.

Monster: a website on which to find and post jobs. Example: Mike found his most recent position on Monster.

Indeed: a website on which to find and post jobs. Example: The CEO posted an ad on Indeed when she was looking for a new executive assistant.

prioritize: to place things in order from most important to least important. Example: There was so much to do before the holiday break, I had to prioritize my to-do list so I knew what to work on first.

Vocabulary Crossword

Complete the crossword below using the vocabulary you just learned.

ACROSS

2. The price that needs to be paid for a headhunter is the _____.

4. If something is _____ school, the idea has been used for a long time.

5. If there are many jobs available, that means there are many job _____.

8. This is a website where you can find jobs.

9. Make sure to _____ your résumé after it has been proofread.

10. I like the idea of meeting someone in person or face-to-_____ to learn about the job.

DOWN

1. This person charges money to help you find a job.

3. You should have a friend read over or do some _____ of your résumé.

6. It is a good idea to figure out what you really want from the job, or to _____.

7. You should update your _____ when applying for jobs.

(Answers are on page 249.)

Idioms Related to Finding Work

Idioms are expressions people use that do not make sense when you translate them word for word. Let's review the following work-related idioms to learn what they mean.

work your fingers to the bone	work very hard
work through something	take your time to get something done
all in a day's work	doing all parts of a task as expected, even if it is difficult or out of the ordinary for most people
do the dirty work	complete a task that is not fun
works for me	that sounds good to me
do your homework	prepare yourself
work against the clock	hurry up to do a task because the time is limited
worked up	be anxious or worried about something
works like magic	it does a good job, such as a cleaner that cleans very well
busywork	a task that is not very important

STOP AND THINK 2

Fill in the blanks using the idioms you just learned.

1. She was able to get the job done, even though some parts were difficult. It was _____ .

2. You should do the job very quickly because you need to _____ .

3. He was asked to do all the work that nobody wanted to do. He did the _____ .

4. Before you go to that interview, you need to research the company, or _____ .

5. You always work long hours every day of the week. You _____ .

6. That sounds like a great idea. That _____ .

7. If you keep working, you should be able to get it done. You just have to _____ .

8. Some employers give their employees a lot to do that is not that important. You can call it _____ .

9. You don't need to worry about that because it is going to be okay. There is no need to get _____ .

10. If you look through those job search websites carefully, you should be able to find a job of interest. It _____ .

(Answers are on page 249.)

THE INTERVIEW

Finding the right job to apply for is important, but preparing for the interview is just as important. The following story talks about how Sofia prepared for her interview. Read the story and answer the questions that follow.

Sofia found a few jobs she wanted to apply for but was not sure what to wear to the interview. She looked online for ideas. She found out that she should dress conservatively since she was looking for a corporate job. She also learned that it was very important to get there on time, so she made sure to leave extra early so she could arrive a few minutes before the interview. She also found out that even though she had emailed her résumé, she should bring a copy along to give to her potential employer just in case they did not print it out—and to show she was prepared!

The night before the interview, Sofia made sure to set two alarm clocks just in case one did not go off. It was a good thing she did that because she actually set one to go off at 6 o'clock at night instead of in the morning! She was feeling very good about being over prepared. She also looked at the company's website and found out what their mission or goals were so that she could talk about how she could help them with that. Since she did her homework, she was ready for the interview.

1. What did Sofia look up online?
   - **A.** What to wear
   - **B.** The mission of the company
   - **C.** Both of the above

2. How should she dress for the interview?
   - **A.** In shorts and a T-shirt
   - **B.** Conservatively
   - **C.** Any way she wants

3. Why is it a good idea to bring the résumé to the interview?
   - **A.** To look prepared
   - **B.** In case the employer does not have it
   - **C.** Both of the above

4. What did she learn about the company online?
   - **A.** The names of the staff
   - **B.** The mission of the company
   - **C.** The rules for employees

(Answers are on page 249.)

dress conservatively: wearing professional looking clothes, such as a suit, a skirt that falls below the knee, and dark or neutral colors. Example: When you go to an office job interview, you should dress conservatively.

corporate: relating to a large company. Example: Jobs in a corporate office can be very competitive because many people might apply for the same job.

mission: the overall purpose of a company or organization. Example: You should find out the mission of the place you want to work at before the interview so that you can talk about it with your potential boss.

goals: something you strive to accomplish. Example: It's important to set professional goals each year so you have something to work toward.

When was the last time you looked for a job? Did you follow any of the tips that Sofia found online in the preceding story? Tell us what you did and how you might do it differently next time. Use three or more of the idioms and vocabulary from this chapter in your writing.

_____

_____

_____

_____

_____

_____

(Answers will vary.)

More Idioms Related to Work

There are many work-related idioms. Below you will learn some more commonly used ones. As you read them, think about whether you have ever heard them. Then, complete the crossword puzzle using these idioms.

line of work	a type of work, such as in education or finance
burn your bridges	to get into an argument with someone, making it hard to have a relationship with them again. (For example, if you yell at your boss and say you quit, you probably won't be able to get your job back because you have burned your bridges.)
the bottom line	what absolutely needs to be done to achieve a goal
talk shop	talk about work
red tape	the multiple rules that need to be followed to get something done
swamped	have a lot to do
call the shots	make decisions
learn the ropes	learn about the job
on the back burner	waiting to do a certain task while you do something more important
get your foot in the door	to be able to get an interview or take a less advanced job at a certain place so that you can eventually get the job you want there. (This is similar to the idiom "work your way up the ladder.")

Idiom Crossword

Complete the crossword below using the idioms you just learned.

ACROSS

3. You can call everyone back in the morning. Put that on the back ____ for now.

4. If you are able to get the assistant manager job to get your foot in the ____, that would be good.

5. The boss is the one that gets to call the ____.

6. What really needs to get done, the bottom ____, is the part that is due tomorrow.

8. He had so much work to do that he was just ____.

DOWN

1. Since she is new, she needs to learn the ____.

2. In your line of ____ as a lawyer, you should dress conservatively.

3. If you get into arguments at work you might burn your ____ with some important people.

5. We went to dinner with two people from work and all they did was talk ____.

7. It takes time to get things done when there is a lot of red ____ .

(Answers are on page 249.)

DIALOGUE 3

Listen to and read the following dialogue. Underline all of the vocabulary and idioms from this chapter.

Juan: There are so many job opportunities on Monster and Indeed. It's hard to decide where to apply.

Sofia: I found some ideas on LinkedIn that I am going to research more.

Juan: I would like to get to know some of the people in the companies first.

Sofia: That might be hard to do unless they give you time to talk to them beyond the interview.

Juan: I hope I get a few interviews this week. Thank you for helping me edit my résumé. I think it'll stand out with that cool template I used.

Sofia: Yeah, it really does look great! I think I should continue to work on mine, though.

Juan: We can always improve the writing and format!

Sofia: Well, there's no reason to worry about yours, because I think you are ready to go.

Juan: I hope we can get through the red tape and get great jobs soon!

Sofia: If you could at least get your foot in the door, that would be super.

Chapter Reflection

The following is a summary of what was covered in this chapter, from searching for a job, to fixing your résumé, to going on an interview. Practice interviewing with a friend before going on your next job interview. Start by writing down questions you think they might ask and prepare your answers so you are ready.

Vocabulary

opportunities	template	Indeed
firsthand	classifieds	prioritize
LinkedIn	old school	dress conservatively
Résumé	headhunter	corporate
edit	recruiter	mission
proofreading	fee	goals
format	face-to-face	
stand out	Monster	

Idioms

work your fingers to the bone	line of work
work through something	burn your bridges
all in a day's work	the bottom line
do the dirty work	talk shop
works for me	red tape
do your homework	swamped
work against the clock	call the shots
worked up	learn the ropes
works like magic	on the back burner
busywork	get your foot in the door

Do you remember all of the information we covered in this chapter? If not, go back and review it to make sure you do. Practice vocabulary and idioms in your conversations, and look for them when you are reading different materials. In addition, look online at one of the websites, such as *indeed.com*, to look into job opportunities. You might just find a new one for yourself. If you do, work on your résumé to make it stand out, and follow the other tips from this chapter to get that job!

CHAPTER 9

Going to School

After reading this chapter, you should know more about . . .

- **Finding the right school**
- **Paying for school**
- **Succeeding in school**
- **Vocabulary related to going to school, such as:**
    - Acceptance rate
    - Financial aid
    - Transcript

What School Will You Go to?

Finding the best school for you can be hard, but in the end, it will be worth your while. If you take the time to look into different schools to find out what aid they offer, what sports they have, what clubs you can join, what academic programs they offer, and who goes to them, you are on your way to finding the perfect school for you. The academic part of school is the most important, but you also want to make connections with other students and faculty while you are there. That is why looking into what clubs are available is a great idea.

DIALOGUE 1

Let's see what John and Jessica said about finding a school.

Jessica: When I go to college, I want to stay close to my house.

John: I don't mind going away. In fact, I think it would be great to go to another state.

Jessica: Well, I don't want to live in a dorm with strangers.

John: I don't mind that. The only problem is that if you go to school out of state, the tuition is a lot higher, unless you get a scholarship or grant or something. Plus you have to pay for room and board.

Jessica: I don't want to get into too much debt.

John: Yeah, but it would be neat to go far, like New York or Utah.

Jessica: Would you ever go to a school in another country?

John: I don't know about that.

Jessica: That can be even more expensive, depending on where you go.

John: Well, for now I want to do some research about nearby schools. How will you pay for school? Are you looking at getting financial aid?

Jessica: I don't know. I want to talk to a guidance counselor to see what advice they can give me.

faculty: the teachers at a college or university. Example: The faculty at a university can help students in class and also during office hours.

dorm: the shortened word for dormitory, which is a building where many college students live. Example: Miguel would rather live at home than in a dorm to save money.

out-of-state: when you are from a state other than the one the school is located in. Example: Out-of-state students can come from nearby and also from very far.

tuition: the money you need to pay to take classes. Example: The tuition at most universities continues to increase every year.

scholarship: a monetary award you can apply for (or be awarded) to help you pay for school; it can be based on your grades or skills (sports, clubs, etc.). Example: If Emma gets a big scholarship to help pay for school, she can save a lot of money.

grant: money you might receive to help you pay for school if you have financial need, such as a Pell Grant from the government; you apply for grants like you do scholarships. Example: Josh will try to get a grant in addition to getting a scholarship.

room and board: expenses related to dining on campus and living in campus housing. Example: The room and board at that university is more expensive than any others Sarah looked at.

research: look into a topic to find an answer (by reading online, calling, or talking to someone face-to-face who knows the answer). Example: She

needs to do some research to find a university that she can afford.

financial aid: federal help to pay for school; you need to fill out a Free Application for Federal Student Aid (FAFSA) form to see if you qualify. Example: Mariana thought it was a very good idea to look into the possibility of financial aid.

guidance counselor: a person who can give you tips about going to college and how to succeed. Example: Jake talked to his guidance counselor to help him figure out where he might want to go after high school.

WRITE IT DOWN

Think about a plan for going to college. What steps are you going to take? Write them down here.

_____

_____

_____

_____

_____

_____

(Answers will vary.)

STOP AND THINK

Look at dialogue 1 and underline the parts that you think will be most challenging or difficult for you. Then, talk to a friend about how you might work them out.

Look at the following sentences and write down whether they are TRUE or FALSE.

_____ **1.** Everyone can get financial aid.

_____ **2.** In order to go to college, you need to pay tuition.

_____ **3.** The faculty members at a college teach the courses.

_____ **4.** A dorm is where the faculty live.

_____ **5.** You should do some research before picking a school.

_____ **6.** Room and board are what you pay for a place to live and for dining on campus.

_____ **7.** A guidance counselor can solve all of your problems.

_____ **8.** Out-of-state tuition can be very expensive.

_____ **9.** A scholarship can help you pay for school.

(Answers are on page 249.)

Researching Schools

Finding out about schools is easy if you do your research online. For example, just look at the website *mycollegeoptions.org* to see a list of schools in your area. For Cleveland, Ohio, it says that there are 24 colleges just in that area. If you look at the whole state of Ohio, there are 218 colleges and universities. That is a lot to research! Another idea is to do a search on "best colleges in graphic design" or for the field you plan to study, which can help narrow down your search.

DIALOGUE 2

How are John and Jessica going to find out about schools? Let's see!

Jessica: Hey, John, have you looked into which college you want to go to yet?

John: I'd like to go to college for computer engineering. I'm thinking I'll stay close by after all, though.

Jessica: I've done a lot of research, and it looks like I don't qualify for much financial aid. So, I'm looking at going to the community college for the first two years before transferring to a four-year institution.

John: That's not a bad idea. I was thinking about that, too. As much as I want to get into a university now, it might save me thousands of dollars to go to the community college first.

Jessica: The other idea I had was to see if I could get a debate scholarship. If that helped pay for school, I could go to a four-year university from the start.

John: All these choices and decisions are overwhelming.

Jessica: After I talked to a guidance counselor, I felt much better. You might want to try that.

John: Maybe I'll call one tomorrow.

Jessica: Let's keep in touch about our progress.

John: Yeah, it helps keep me on track.

college: an institution of higher learning or a group or section at a university focused on a specific field, such as the college of business or nursing. Example: She will be studying in the college of education to become a teacher.

university: an institution of higher learning made up of a number of colleges. Example: That university has seven different colleges.

community college: a two-year college, which can be cheaper than a four-year college, that most anyone can attend. Example: Since Sam is on a budget and didn't get a scholarship, he is considering going to a community college first.

transferring: withdrawing from one school to enroll at another school. Example: Since Kate knows she will be transferring, she is making sure she only takes classes that will transfer her credits to the new school.

four-year institution: a college that has a four-year degree program. Example: Maria just graduated from a four-year institution with her bachelor's degree in nursing.

keep in touch: an idiom that means let's talk again. Example: After spending their college years together and graduating at the same time, Dan and Tim said, "Let's keep in touch."

keep me on track: an idiom that means something will help you achieve your goals. Example: I like to study with my friend because she will keep me on track.

WRITE IT DOWN

Have you thought about researching schools? What three things are most important to you when looking for a school? Write them down here, and compare with a friend. Then, go online to see if you can find a school with those things.

_____

_____

_____

_____

_____

_____

(Answers will vary.)

Vocabulary Crossword

Complete the crossword below using the vocabulary you just learned.

ACROSS

3. I need to do some _____ to figure out which school I should attend.

5. The _____ at the university can teach many courses.

6. I plan to go to _____ after high school.

7. I will be _____ from the community college to the university.

9. I need to talk to a guidance _____ for tips about going to school.

10. He wanted to get away. He wanted to go out of _____.

DOWN

1. I would like to stay in a _____ to sleep.

2. If I get federal _____ aid, I will be able to go to school.

4. I hope I get a _____ that would help me pay for school.

8. I can get my two-year degree at the _____ college.

(Answers are on page 249.)

STOP AND THINK

Use the vocabulary and idioms you have learned so far in this chapter to fill in the blanks.

1. He was thinking of going to one school and then later _____ to another school.

2. If you keep in _____ with someone, you likely know how they are doing.

3. The _____ of Education at Johns Hopkins University is one of the best in the nation.

4. Please keep me on _____ because I want to finish college in four years.

5. A four-year _____ is a college that has a four-year degree, such as a bachelor's degree in biology.

6. At a _____ college you can get a two-year degree, or an associate's degree.

(Answers are on page 249.)

Getting into School

Deciding you want to go to school is the first step. However, getting into school can be a challenge if you pick a school with a low acceptance rate. You should keep in mind what you want to study and how much money you are willing to spend. Sometimes less is more.

DIALOGUE 3

What are John and Jessica doing to get into the school of their choice? Let's see!

John: I've decided to go to a university near here. I am going to bite the bullet and just pay for it if I don't get financial aid or any scholarships. I don't want to bother transferring, and I think I'll save money by staying in the same state.

Jessica: Have you applied yet? What do they require?

John: They need my SAT scores, an essay, and my high school transcript.

Jessica: Have you studied for the SAT yet?

John: Yeah, I've been studying. I got a test-prep book on Amazon.

Jessica: I'm going to the community college first. That way I can save some money. I noticed there are some debate teams in the area, so I will probably go to one of those schools.

John: Well, you don't have to worry about the SAT then, right?

Jessica: No, I don't think so. The university just asks you for your college transcripts.

John: One less thing for you to worry about!

Jessica: They do have a placement test at the community college, though. So I want to do well on that test so I don't have to take any remedial classes.

John: I bet you will do just fine if you study. Let's hit the books.

acceptance rate: the number of students who get into a university out of the number who applied. Example: The acceptance rate at that university is 40 percent.

less is more: an idiom that means spending less or doing less can be better in the end. Example: When a professor asks for a three- to five-page paper, you should not write more than that because less is more.

bite the bullet: an idiom that means doing something that can be hard or unpleasant. Example: She will bite the bullet and get her paper written this weekend.

SAT: a test that shows your reading, writing, and math skills. Many high school students study for the SAT so they get a good score to help them get into college.

transcript: a record of grades. Example: Alicia's transcript was outstanding—all A's.

test-prep book: a book that helps you prepare for a standardized test. Example: Ajai bought a test-prep book for the SAT to help him study on his own.

remedial classes: classes that help you prepare for college-level classes; for example, remedial reading classes help you understand how to read college textbooks. Example: Students who have trouble reading might be required to take remedial classes.

hit the books: an idiom that means to start studying. Example: He would like to hit the books early so that he can have some fun later.

WRITE IT DOWN

Write a sentence for each of the following vocabulary words or idioms.

less is more: _____

acceptance rate: _____

bite the bullet: _____

hit the books: _____

remedial classes: _____

test-prep book: _____

SAT: _____

transcript: _____

(Answers will vary.)

Extracurricular Activities

Have you ever been involved in extracurricular activities, such as the Spanish club or math team? You might consider looking into what clubs they have at the college you will be attending. All colleges have activities that you can join in or watch. There might be plays, art shows, debates, lectures, film festivals, affinity groups, or other clubs you can join to get to know people in your new school.

DIALOGUE 4

Let's see what clubs Jessica and John are considering.

John: I hope they have a future engineers' club at the university I picked.

Jessica: I'm going to find out if they have a speech or debate group.

John: It would be interesting to see if they have a lot of free events, too.

Jessica: Yeah. I will be looking into freebies as much as possible, since I won't have too much money after paying for school.

John: Let me know about your school's events, and I will let you know about mine.

Jessica: Absolutely! I heard they also have music and comedy shows. This is going to be great!

John: I am really excited.

Jessica: Once we are in, though, we need to be serious and not skip class.

John: I heard you can skip a few classes.

Jessica: Maybe a few, but too many and we won't pass with flying colors.

John: We just need the right balance between studying and having fun.

Jessica: Yes!

lectures: talks that provide information or teach something. Example: Professor DiGuerra has some very interesting lectures that include many video clips.

affinity group: a group of people with a similar interest who join together to work toward their goals. Example: Students should find out about the affinity groups at their school in order to make connections with people with similar interests.

freebies: things that are free. Example: Sometimes there are freebies during special university events.

skip class: not going to class. Example: It is not a good idea to skip class, especially when there is a grade for attendance.

pass with flying colors: an idiom that means to do very well in a class; for example, getting 100 percent on a test means you've passed with flying colors. Example: Louisa was hoping to pass with flying colors so that her final grade could be an A.

Idioms Related to School

The following idioms are heard in school or out of school, although some of them sound like you would only hear them in school.

"A" for effort	trying very hard to do a good job, but not necessarily doing well
brainstorm	think about ways to solve a problem or create an idea
learn your lesson	to learn how you should not do something by making a mistake
teacher's pet	the teacher's favorite student
fill in the blanks	someone might say this when they don't want to tell you all of the details; they might also use the idiom "read between the lines"
work your way through college	when you have to work while going to college to pay for your education
crank out a paper	get a paper written, usually quickly and without concern for quality
make the grade	do well in something, such as in a job
school of thought	the way people might think about something
the three Rs	another way to say reading, writing, and arithmetic (reading, 'riting, 'rithmetic)

STOP AND THINK

Go back and put a star next to the idioms you already knew and a question mark next to the ones you did not know. How many are new to you? Try to use these in your everyday life to get used to them.

Read the sentences and pick the idiom that best matches each one.

A. "A" for effort

B. Brainstorm

C. Learn your lesson

D. Teacher's pet

E. Fill in the blanks

F. Work your way through college

G. Crank out a paper

H. Make the grade

I. The three R's

1. _____ The teacher just loves Elaine.

2. _____ I need to get that paper written today.

3. _____ She tried very hard to do well, but she did just okay.

4. _____ He told me some information about himself and then said to read between the lines.

5. _____ After failing that test because I did not study enough, I learned to make sure not to do that again.

6. _____ I am working during the day in an office and then going to school at night.

7. _____ We had to think of ways to get her into that school.

8. _____ We learn this in school from the very beginning.

9. _____ She did very well in her work, so she got promoted.

(Answers are on page 249.)

Registering Children in School

If you have a child, how do you go about registering them for school? You should call the main office of the school district and ask when you can go in to register and what you need to bring. You likely will need to bring their birth certificate. They will probably also ask you to bring your driver's license, a utility bill, or something else that proves where you live. When you call, make sure you write down everything, because they will likely tell you lots of information. In addition, find out what services they might have, such as school social workers or government agencies they can recommend to help your child succeed in school.

Once you have registered your child and they begin school, make sure to regularly talk to their teacher to see how you can help. If you notice they are having trouble doing their homework all of the time or they tell you they can't do the work in class, make sure to share that information with their teacher. The teacher might have the same concerns. You should tell the teacher you would like your child tested to see if they qualify for extra help with an Individualized Education Plan (IEP). For example, your child might need extra help in math or reading, or maybe they need extra help to focus in class. You can also talk to the school principal about the testing process. Show support for your child by talking to their teacher or principal today!

school social workers: people who help with problems students might have, such as with their grades, mental health, or economic issues. Example: The school social worker met with the family to help them work out a plan for better home–school communication.

WRITE IT DOWN

Look online to find what basic things you need to bring when registering a child in school. Write a list of them here. Then, look at your local school's website and find out what services they might be able to provide.

_____

_____

_____

_____

_____

_____

_____

_____

_____

(Answers will vary.)

Chapter Reflection

The following is a summary of what was covered in this chapter, from finding the right school and paying for school to helping your own child succeed in school. Look at different universities' websites to see how they compare after you have made yourself a list of everything you want in a school.

Vocabulary

faculty	financial aid	SAT
dorm	guidance counselor	transcript
out-of-state	college	test-prep book
tuition	university	remedial classes
scholarship	community college	lectures
grant	transferring	affinity group
room and board	four-year institution	freebies
research	acceptance rate	school social workers

Idioms

keep in touch	learn your lesson
keep me on track	teacher's pet
less is more	fill in the blanks
bite the bullet	work your way through college
hit the books	crank out a paper
skip class	make the grade
pass with flying colors	school of thought
"A" for effort	the three R's
brainstorm	

Do you remember all of the information we covered in this chapter? If not, go back and review it to make sure you do. Practice vocabulary and idioms in your conversations, and look for them when you are reading different materials. Meet with your guidance counselor if you are planning to go to college, and find out what they suggest. Better yet, find a friend to go to a guidance counselor with you so that you can hear the suggestions together and talk about them later. If you have a child or children who are in school, call or email their teachers to get an update on how your child is doing and ask whether there is anything the teacher is concerned about and how you can help.

CHAPTER 10

Staying Safe

After reading this chapter, you should know more about . . .

- **The importance of watching your surroundings**
- **Online security**
- **Vocabulary related to safety, such as the following:**
  - Companion
  - Security software updates
  - Cybercriminals
  - Wi-Fi hotspots

What Can You Do When You're in Public?

There are many ways to avoid being a victim of crime, whether you are in the United States or elsewhere. Even if you are living in the nicest area in the world, crime happens. Whether you are out in public or in your home, criminals can find ways to get you if you give them the opportunity. It is always a good idea to pay attention while you are walking around during the day and at night. It is also helpful to get in your car quickly and not stay in your car for long periods while in an empty parking lot. Criminals look for people who are distracted and alone so that they can easily get what they want. It might be a cell phone, a purse, or a laptop that they see. Anything that looks valuable can be taken if you make it easy for them. In this chapter you will find out some tips for staying safe.

DIALOGUE 1

Let's see what happened to Sofia in the following dialogue.

Sofia: You know what happened to me last night?

Juan: No, what?

Sofia: I got home at about 2 a.m. and couldn't find a parking spot close to my apartment, so I parked a few blocks away. When I started to walk home, I noticed two guys following me.

Juan: What did you do?

Sofia: I crossed the street to see if they would stay on the other side.

Juan: Did they?

Sofia: No, they crossed the street to follow me.

Juan: Oh, no! Then what happened?

Sofia: I crossed the street again and I started running as fast as I could to my apartment.

Juan: Did they get you?

Sofia: No, thank goodness.

Juan: That's a relief!

Sofia: I think they were muggers, but it could have been worse. What if they were kidnappers? I don't even want to think about that.

Juan: You were lucky. You should probably try to walk with a companion if possible.

Sofia: I guess you are right. It's just that if I am coming home alone, I don't have anyone.

Juan: Well, being aware of your surroundings, just like you were, is a good idea.

Sofia: If I were on my phone texting or talking, I might not have noticed them.

Juan: I'm so glad you're okay.

> **criminal:** a person who does not follow the law. Example: She is a criminal who likes to steal credit cards from people.
>
> **mugger:** a person who steals from others in public; they may take items such as your purse, wallet, or cell phone. Example: The mugger took her purse and then ran away quickly.

kidnapper: a person who holds another person against his or her will, many times to get money (ransom) from the family and friends of the victim in exchange for his or her return, or to hold him or her hostage as their prisoner. Example: The kidnapper wanted $500,000 in return for the little boy.

companion: a friend or animal who spends time with you. Example: A dog is a good companion for going on walks.

surroundings: the immediate area around you. Example: She always watches her surroundings when going for a run.

WRITE IT DOWN

Have you had a similar experience to Sofia's? Write about it and tell us how you have avoided that type of situation since then. If you haven't, write down some steps you can take to help prevent this from happening to you.

_____

_____

_____

_____

_____

_____

(Answers will vary.)

Inviting People into Your House

If you are out and meet a kind person, you should not automatically invite them to your house for coffee or anything else until you get to know them better. They might be a **con artist** who wants to take your belongings or steal your identity. **Identity theft** is a real issue that can take months to fix, so the best thing is to prevent it. It can happen by someone taking your name, email address, home address, social security number, birthdate, driver's license number, and/or other information so that they can pretend to be you to use your credit cards or bank account. It can be helpful to check your credit report to look for activity you haven't done yourself. However, sometimes criminals take advantage of you even if you are careful. What are some things you can do if you are a victim? Fill in the following true and false questions, and check your answers in the back of the book to see how much you know.

TRUE OR FALSE

_____ **1.** You should contact the Federal Trade Commission for help if you think your identity has been stolen.

_____ **2.** It takes about one month to fix the problems related to having your identity stolen.

_____ **3.** If you have been paying your bills on time for years, it might be easier to prove you had your identity stolen.

_____ **4.** You should not let your bank and credit card companies know that you suspect you are a victim of identity theft.

_____ **5.** If you think your identity has been stolen, you should file a fraud alert.

_____ **6.** If you think your identity has been stolen, you should file a police report.

_____ **7.** If you think your identity has been stolen, you should change all of your passwords to your accounts.

_____ **8.** If you think your identity has been stolen, you don't need to get a new driver's license.

_____ **9.** If you think your identity has been stolen, you don't need to call your electric or phone company.

_____ **10.** You should monitor your credit reports.

(Answers are on page 249.)

con artist: a person who tries to trick you in order to get your money. Example: You should not bring him to your house because he is a con artist.

identity theft: when your personal information is stolen, such as your social security number, and the information is used to buy things or spend money in your name. Example: Identity theft can be very time consuming because you have to prove you did not make the purchases made by someone else.

MATCHING

Match the following words to their definitions using the vocabulary you just learned.

A. Criminal
B. Mugger
C. Companion
D. Identity theft
E. Surroundings
F. Con artist
G. Kidnapper

1. _____ a friend or animal who spends time with you

2. _____ a person who does not follow the law

3. _____ a person who steals from others in public; they may take items such as your purse, wallet, or cell phone

4. _____ when your personal information is stolen, such as your social security number, and the information is used to buy things or spend money in your name

5. _____ the immediate area around you

6. _____ a person who tries to trick you out of your money

7. _____ a person who holds another person against his or her will, many times to get money (ransom) from the family and friends of the victim in exchange for his or her return, or to hold him or her hostage as their prisoner

(Answers are on page 249.)

Idioms Related to Crime

There are many idioms that remind us that crime is not a good way to live your life. However, there are idioms that sound like they are about crime, but they really are not. Look at the following idioms, and circle the ones that you have not heard before now.

crime doesn't pay	crime ultimately will not benefit someone
partners in crime	two people who do something they shouldn't be doing, which may or may not be illegal
better safe than sorry	it is better to stop something from happening than it is to deal with it after it has happened
highway robbery	when someone charges way too much for something, but you feel like you have to pay it
scream bloody murder	yell loudly or protest
on the run	someone running away from something
a steal	when the price for something is so good it seems like you are stealing it
a hot car	a stolen car
behind bars	in jail
get off easy	get a punishment that is not too bad
get away with something	do something wrong without getting caught
face the music	to get in trouble for something you did wrong
go by the book	follow the rules

STOP AND THINK

Fill in the blanks with the most appropriate idiom from the list above.

1. She is my _____ in crime because we always stay up way too late together.

2. The truth is that crime doesn't _____ . You are better off following the law.

3. He was on the _____ ever since he robbed the bank.

4. That is a _____ car. We need to tell the police.

5. That was such a _____ .
I couldn't believe how cheap it was to get those shoes.

6. Put your raincoat on because it is about to rain heavily. You don't want to be wet all day. It is better to be safe than _____ .

7. He was screaming bloody _____ at the cashier because he didn't get the discounted price he thought he was going to get.

8. My car broke down, and the price the mechanic charged me amounted to highway _____ .

9. She is behind _____ because she stole someone's identity.

10. You shouldn't think you could get away with _____ , because there are cameras everywhere.

11. She will probably get off _____ because this was her first time committing a crime.

12. Be prepared to face the _____ if you steal something.

13. That teacher is very strict and will go by the _____ .

(Answers are on page 249.)

STORY TIME

ONLINE SECURITY

Online security was important to Juan because he wanted to keep his identity safe. He regularly updated his passwords and did not use his birthday or social security number in them. He also regularly did *security software updates*. He was worried about *cybercriminals* and had heard that if you use a *Wi-Fi hotspot* without a password you could open yourself to *hackers*. His friend Sofia thought he was too paranoid. Juan didn't care because he would rather be safe than sorry. As it turns out, somehow his credit card number was stolen and used in a few stores. The thief spent about $800 that month in his name. When Juan got his credit card bill, he could not believe it had happened to him. He was always so careful. He called the credit card company and explained that the purchases were not his, and they were removed after he answered many questions. He still does not know how a thief got his credit card number, but he feels lucky that more than that was not stolen.

1. Was Juan too careful about identity theft?
   A. No
   B. Yes

2. Did Juan get robbed even though he was careful?
   A. No
   B. Yes

3. How did a hacker get his credit card information?
   A. Juan used a Wi-Fi hotspot.
   B. Juan left his credit card information at work.
   C. The story did not explain how it was stolen.

4. Are security software updates supposed to help you?
   A. No
   B. Yes

5. Why is online security important?
   A. To prevent hackers from getting your information.
   B. To help Google.
   C. To make sure your friends can reach you.

(Answers are on page 249.)

Have you or do you know someone who has had their identity stolen? What are some things you or they can do to avoid it in the future? Look ideas up on Google, then write them down, and talk about it with a friend.

_____

_____

_____

_____

_____

_____

(Answers will vary.)

Learning About Security

There are many websites with tips to help you learn about online security. For example, McAfee, which also provides an antivirus program, has a page with great information. Other useful websites with information about online safety include the National Cyber Security Alliance and Cnet. Here are a few tips to keep yourself secure: use a strong password (which means a long password with uppercase and lowercase letters and numbers that cannot easily be figured out by hackers); do not open up links sent to you in an email from a stranger; and do not send personal information through emails (such as your social security number).

online security: guarding against crime on the Internet, such as someone stealing your credit card number. Example: She was very careful about online security, which is why she didn't like looking at her accounts while she was at Starbucks.

security software updates: updates that bring your computer up to date to keep it from getting viruses. Example: Ever since he got a virus on his computer, he has made sure to do any security software updates available.

cybercriminal: a person who uses the computer to break the law, such as by hacking. Example: It is a shame that we have to worry about cybercriminals when we are on the Internet.

Wi-Fi hotspot: a place where people can get wireless Internet access. Example: Many restaurants have a Wi-Fi hotspot for their customers.

hacker: a person who illegally gains access to a computer system to get information to cause harm or steal. Example: He went to prison for being a hacker.

Juan and Sofia went to a class to learn how to be safe online. Listen to and read the following dialogue to hear about what they learned. Underline any idioms you see.

Sofia: That class was pretty good. I never knew the importance of not having the same password for all of your accounts.

Juan: Yeah, I have to go and change my passwords.

Sofia: It's so hard to have them all different though, because how can you remember them?

Juan: I know! That's what I was thinking!

Sofia: I was happy to hear they are catching more cybercriminals now. Crime doesn't pay.

Juan: But it sounds like many of them are still on the run. Hey, what did you think about not using public Wi-Fi hotspots for your online banking?

Sofia: I never felt comfortable doing my banking in public because I didn't want people near me to see my bank information. Now that I know it is not safe, I definitely won't do it.

Juan: I wish all cybercriminals could be behind bars.

Sofia: Well, we learned that it is hard to catch them, so we need to be careful and not leave ourselves open to them.

Juan: I also need to be more careful about not using my credit card in Wi-Fi hotspots. It's hard, though, because sometimes I want to buy something online while I'm at a restaurant with a hotspot.

Sofia: Being safe can be annoying, but it is better to be safe than sorry.

How many idioms did you find? _____

(Answers are on page 249.)

Let's see how good you are at guessing the meaning of the following idioms. Write down what you think they mean, and then check your answers in the answer key at the back of the book.

1. **hand in the cookie jar** _____

_____

2. **serve time** _____

_____

(Answers are on page 249.)

How did you do? Now try to use them in your everyday conversations!

Car Safety

It is not a good idea to give strangers a ride, because even though you think you are doing a good deed, they might not be as friendly as you think. They might have a gun and make you go to your bank to withdraw your money, they might steal your car, or they might commit some other crime. Aside from not giving strangers rides, it is a good idea to keep your valuables out of sight in your car. Thieves might be tempted to break a window if they see a bag that might have money in it or another expensive item such as a laptop or cell phone. You also want to make sure you keep your doors locked, even if your car is parked in your driveway.

DIALOGUE 3

Let's hear about Juan and Sofia's car ride in this dialogue.

Juan: Hey, Sofia, let's go to the beach.

Sofia: Sure, Juan! But I have some work to do, so would you mind if, on the way there, I do some work on my laptop?

Juan: That's fine. I borrowed my friend's car while he's away, so I will be driving.

Sofia: Great! I'm ready. You can't beat the price of a free rental. That's a steal!

Juan: Let's go! I am looking forward to relaxing on the beach, but we should still be aware of our surroundings once we get there.

Sofia: Is this a hot car? Just kidding.

Juan: We're here, so let's have fun!

Sofia: Awesome! I'll just leave my bag here on the backseat so I don't have to carry everything.

Juan: Sure, that's fine.

Sofia: On second thought, let me toss it in the trunk. I don't want to invite crime.

Juan: That's a great idea, because I don't want to have to get my friend a new car window, and that would be horrible to get your things stolen.

Sofia: Okay, now let's go have fun!

STOP AND THINK

What vocabulary or idioms do you see in the above dialogue? Go back and circle them.

(Answers are on page 249.)

Chapter Reflection

The following is a summary of what was covered in this chapter, from being safe inside your home to being careful online or out in public. Many ideas were discussed, so hopefully you will follow the tips provided! Check online for ways to be safe so you can learn more.

Vocabulary

criminal	identity theft
mugger	online security
kidnapper	security software updates
companion	cybercriminal
surroundings	Wi-Fi hotspot
con artist	hacker

Idioms

crime doesn't pay	behind bars
partners in crime	hand in the cookie jar
better safe than sorry	serve time
highway robbery	get a slap on the wrist
scream bloody murder	get away with something
on the run	face the music
a steal	get off easy
a hot car	go by the book

Do you remember all of the information covered in this chapter? If not, go back and review it to make sure you do. Practice the vocabulary and idioms in your conversations, and look for them when you are reading different materials. Make sure to change your passwords, update your security software, and leave nothing valuable in your car.

CHAPTER 11

Running Errands

After reading this chapter, you should know more about . . .

- **The post office**
- **Shopping for household items**
- **Dry cleaners**
- **Vocabulary related to running errands, such as the following:**
    - Automate
    - Business hours
    - Snail mail

Free Time

Whenever you have free time, whether it is on the weekend, in the evening, or at some other time, hopefully you balance some time for fun with running errands. Looking forward to being able to do what you want when you want can get you through a rough workweek. With errands, of course, we need to think about when places are open or when they close. For example, many stores close early on Sundays, so if you think you will be shopping after dinner on Sunday, you might want to

check whether the store you want to go to is still open. If you have a smartphone, the OK Google app can help you figure that out very quickly. Just say "OK, Google, at what time does Michael's close today?" and you will find out the answer to your question within seconds. If you don't have a smartphone, look it up online; that can save you from going to the store only to see that it is closed. What are some other typical errands people run? Some of them include going to the bank, the post office, the pharmacy, the library, or the dry cleaners, or going to a doctor or dentist appointment, the vet, or some other appointment. This chapter has lots of advice for getting errands done.

DIALOGUE 1

Let's see how Bob and Tracey spent their Saturday in the following dialogue.

Bob: You better get up, Tracey, because we have a lot to do today.

Tracey: What time is it? Did you really have to call me this early? I was hoping to sleep in.

Bob: Well, if you sleep in, you might not be able to go to the bank like you wanted to. Their business hours are from nine to one today.

Tracey: Thanks for the reminder, and for giving me a ride. We'd better hop to it.

Bob: I'm hoping to go to the library and the dry cleaners and to get my oil changed.

Tracey: Let's start with a good breakfast. How about some scrambled eggs with spinach and cheese?

Bob: Sounds like a good way to get going to me! I'll be right over!

> **errands:** something you need to do, pick up, or drop off, such as going to get your oil changed, picking up a medicine, or dropping off a book at the library. Example: Kacey wanted to run all of her errands on Saturday.
>
> **dry cleaners:** a place that will clean your most delicate clothes using chemicals instead of water. Example: Michael needed to pick up his pants at the dry cleaners.
>
> **vet:** the shortened word for veterinarian, or animal doctor; vet can also be short for veteran, which is a person who served in the military. Example: Suzie used the same vet for all of her pets over the years.

advice: helpful ideas, tips, or recommendations. Example: Carlos wanted advice about which vet to visit.

sleep in: to sleep longer than usual. Example: He likes to sleep in when he is off from work.

business hours: the hours that a business is open. Example: His business hours are from 9 a.m. to 5 p.m.

hop to it: an idiom that means you need to start doing something soon. Example: You should hop to it if you are going to get everything done by 5 p.m.

WRITE IT DOWN

What kinds of errands do you usually run? Write down a typical to-do list on the lines below. Try to use a few vocabulary words from this and earlier chapters.

_____

_____

_____

_____

_____

_____

(Answers will vary.)

Making Errands Easier

Did you know that you can **automate** some of your errands? It can make your life a lot easier if you do. For example, instead of checking out a **paperback book** at the library, you could read books on an **e-reader**. If you do, the books are automatically returned for you when they are due. You can also have **prescriptions** that you need refilled regularly filled automatically through your **health-care provider** or at some stores, such as Walgreens. You could automate purchases on Amazon for things you always need—for example, laundry detergent, toilet paper, and paper towels. You could also buy clothes you don't need to try on through Amazon, such as socks and underwear. Some dry cleaners will pick up and drop off your clothes for you. Last but not least, you could always pay someone to run your errands. There are websites online that tell you all of the types of errands someone can do for you.

automate: to make something happen automatically, or without much effort; Example: Andrea would like to automate some of her errands.

paperback book: a book that has a thick paper cover. Example: I like paperback books because they are lighter than hardcover books.

e-reader: a device that lets you read books, newspapers, and magazines electronically, such as a Nook, Kindle, or iPad. Example: Some people prefer an e-reader to a book because they can have many books on it.

prescription: a doctor's note that allows a person to get certain medications from a drugstore; it also gives instructions on how and when to take the medicine. Example: Stefanie needed a prescription because she had strep throat.

health-care provider: a person who helps identify or prevent illness or injury and then helps treat you, such as a doctor, dentist, nurse, or physical therapist. Example: My health-care provider would like me to stop eating sugar.

TRUE OR FALSE

Let's see how much you remember by completing this true or false quiz.

_____ **1.** You can hire someone to run your errands for you.

_____ **2.** If you sleep in on a Saturday, some places might close before you get there.

_____ **3.** If you hop to it, you will be doing it very soon.

_____ **4.** If you read library e-books, they will automatically be returned when they are due.

_____ **5.** You cannot get things delivered to your house, such as laundry detergent, socks, and underwear, through Amazon.

_____ **6.** You could get your prescriptions refilled automatically through some stores.

_____ **7.** Vet is a short way to say veterinarian or veteran.

_____ **8.** When you automate your errands, it takes longer to do them.

_____ **9.** A doctor is a health-care provider.

(Answers are on page 249.)

Let's see what Bob and Tracey think about automating their errands.

Tracey: Have you thought about buying things online on Amazon?

Bob: Yeah, but I haven't done it because you have to spend at least $50 to get free delivery, unless you pay for Amazon Prime, but that costs $99 a year. I try to just buy things as I need them so that I don't have to pay a lot of money at once.

Tracey: I was doing that, too, but then it felt like I was always running errands. It was annoying.

Bob: Maybe if we're organized and budget ourselves, we can figure out how to automate some of our **purchases**.

Tracey: Now it just seems complicated.

Bob: Well, it would be cheaper than hiring someone to run our errands.

Tracey: I hadn't even considered that idea. That's probably expensive.

Bob: There's money to be made there!

Tracey: How much does a person who runs errands make?

Bob: I hear it can be between $20 and $40 an hour, plus a fee for **mileage**, and they usually charge extra for holidays or **after-hours**.

Tracey: That's not bad! Maybe we should start our own business.

Bob: I thought we were trying to run fewer errands, not more errands!

Tracey: Ha ha, you're right.

purchases: items you buy. Example: You should try not to make too many purchases over the holidays or you might get into debt.

mileage: the number of miles it takes to drive somewhere. Example: He was able to track his mileage using Google Maps.

after-hours: the time after business hours. Example: Madison would like to go there after-hours, but the doctor said he would be gone by then.

Vocabulary Crossword

Complete the crossword below using the vocabulary you just learned.

ACROSS

1. I can use _____ about getting my errands done quickly.

6. I can get my _____ filled automatically at some stores.

8. I have many _____ to do, such as going to the library, post office, and dentist.

9. I can wash most of my clothes in the washer so I don't need to go to the dry _____ very much.

DOWN

1. People usually charge more _____ hours for their services.

2. If I read my books on an _____ I don't have to worry about returning them on time.

3. I would like to _____ my errands so that they happen automatically.

4. You can go there during their _____ hours when it is open.

5. I need to take my dog to the _____ today. I think he is sick.

7. I try not to make more _____ than I need because I don't have a lot of money.

(Answers are on page 250.)

Idioms Related to Errands

There are some idioms that are directly about or can be related to errands. Look at the following idioms, and try to figure out what they mean. Write down your guesses and check the answer key at the back of the book to see if you are right.

1. burn the candle at both ends

_____

2. taskmaster

_____

3. to break even

_____

4. Jack of all trades

_____

5. back to the grind

_____

6. break your back

_____

7. last resort

_____

8. sail through

_____

9. take it easy

_____

10. pain in the neck

_____

(Answers are on page 250.)

STOP AND THINK

Fill in the blanks with the most appropriate idiom you just learned.

1. I need to get back to the _____ so that I can finish my errands by 3 p.m.

2. He is a _____ of all trades and can do many things, including errands, cleaning the house, and cooking.

3. She is exhausting herself burning the candle at both _____ .

4. As a _____ resort he went to a third store hoping to get his favorite cereal.

5. She was able to _____ through the errands today because the stores were empty.

6. He should not do too many errands if he doesn't feel well. He should take it _____ .

7. She was a _____ . She made her children do all of the chores.

8. He was able to _____ even after going shopping and spending his entire paycheck.

9. Try not to break your _____ doing too many errands today.

(Answers are on page 250.)

RUNNING ERRANDS

As much as Bob looked forward to the weekends, he did not look forward to running errands. One weekend he decided he was just going to take it easy and skip his errands. He enjoyed sleeping in, watching television, and eating without having to break his back for a change. The only problem was that on Monday, when it was time to go to work, he didn't have any food to take for lunch. Then, when it was lunch time, he didn't have any money because he did not go to the bank either. He had to rush to an ATM to get some money, buy a quick lunch, and then make it back to work in time. However, he was exhausted after doing all of that in less than half an hour. He was kicking himself for not having gone to the store over the weekend, so on his way home from work, he made sure to stop at the store so that he would not repeat the same mistake the next day. He decided that even though it was a pain in the neck to run errands every weekend, errands should not be skipped.

1. Why did Bob skip running errands?
   - **A.** He was tired of running errands.
   - **B.** He wanted to watch a football game on television.
   - **C.** He was counting on Tracey to run the errands.

2. What does it mean that he was kicking himself?
   - **A.** He kicked himself because he was mad.
   - **B.** He kicked himself by accident.
   - **C.** He was mad at himself for not doing the errands.

3. How much time did Bob have for lunch at work?
   - **A.** One hour
   - **B.** Half an hour
   - **C.** 45 minutes

4. Will Bob skip running errands again?
   - **A.** Yes
   - **B.** No
   - **C.** We do not know for sure based on the story.

5. What is another way to say a pain in the neck?
   - **A.** A noodle
   - **B.** Annoying
   - **C.** Helpful

(Answers are on page 250.)

The Post Office

Who uses the **postal service** when you can pay your bills online or send someone an email instead of a letter? People don't need to write paper letters and send them with a stamp. They also don't need to write their bills and send them in the mail. However, sometimes you do want to send a thank you card or pay certain bills using **snail mail**, so for that reason, you might need to buy stamps and send out some mail in the traditional way. However, you can buy stamps online. What are the reasons left for going to the post office? People go to a post office to send and pick up packages, to send things via **express mail**, to get their **passports**, or to make sure their mail is stamped with today's date to make sure people know they sent something in on time, such as their taxes.

postal service: the government department that sends, receives, and delivers mail; sells stamps and mailing materials; and provides passports. Example: The postal service is getting fewer customers than it used to get.

snail mail: sending something through regular mail instead of through email. Example: Many people prefer email over snail mail.

express mail: mail that is sent more quickly than usual for an added fee. Example: If you really need to get it there in a day, you should send it via express mail.

passport: a form of identification provided by the government that allows people to travel to other countries. Example: He has never gotten a passport even though he is 60 years old.

DIALOGUE 3

Read this dialogue to see how Bob and Tracey use the post office.

Bob: I barely go to the post office. Do you?

Tracey: I go to send out my Christmas cards, but I think I'm going to start sending **e-cards** because stamps are getting expensive.

Bob: I go sometimes to send things through express mail, but that's not often.

Tracey: Did you know we can get our passports at the post office? Do you have your passport?

Bob: No. I used to, but it expired.

Tracey: Maybe we should go to get our passports.

Bob: I've been thinking about that. It's good to have one.

Tracey: We should so that we can travel to another country.

Bob: Okay, and let's start saving money and planning a trip!

e-card: a greeting card that is sent electronically. Example: She sent her thank you card as an e-card.

Do you know about the services the post office provides? If not, look on *USPS.com* and find out. Then, write about how you might use the post office here.

_____

_____

_____

_____

_____

_____

(Answers will vary.)

Chapter Reflection

The following is a summary of what was covered in this chapter, from tips for when and how to run errands to going to the post office. Will you be automating some of your errands? What might you want to automate and why? Share your ideas with a friend. Hopefully this chapter has made you think about ways to make running errands easier for you.

Vocabulary

errands	paperback book	postal service
dry cleaners	e-reader	snail mail
vet	prescription	express mail
advice	health-care provider	passport
sleep in	purchases	e-card
business hours	mileage	
automate	after-hours	

Idioms

hop to it	break your back
burn the candle at both ends	last resort
taskmaster	sail through
to break even	take it easy
Jack of all trades	pain in the neck
back to the grind	

Do you remember all of the information covered in this chapter? If not, go back and review it to make sure you do. Practice vocabulary and idioms in your conversations, and look for them when you are reading different materials. Make sure to run your errands during your free time so that you don't end up like Bob, rushing through your lunch time at work.

CHAPTER 12

The Weather

After reading this chapter, you should know more about . . .

- **Different types of weather, such as sunny versus rainy or cold versus hot**
- **Vocabulary and terms related to weather, such as the following:**
    - Meteorologist
    - Hurricane
    - The Weather Channel

Why Does Everyone Talk About the Weather?

Everyone has to deal with the weather, so it's a topic that you know you can instantly discuss with anyone. Whether it is rainy, sunny, windy, cold, or hot, we can all relate to it and can have an easy conversation

about it. It seems like a good way to break the ice without having to worry about being controversial. If the weather were always the same, it might seem silly to talk about it, but because we have some variety with the seasons in the United States, there is always something to talk about. And, if you are from somewhere that has a different type of weather, you can always add that to the conversation, too. The best part is that you do not have to prepare too much to have a conversation about the weather. All you have to do is step outside for a second and you are ready to go. You could also watch the Weather Channel to see the meteorologist give the forecast, or ask OK Google, "What is the weather like today?"

DIALOGUE 1

Let's see what Jessica and John thought about staying home because of the weather in this dialogue.

Jessica: I'm getting so sick of the rain.

John: We need it, though. Did you know there are some parts of the country in a drought right now?

Jessica: Yeah, but I want to be able to go outside without my umbrella.

John: It *is* rainy season.

Jessica: I know. I just don't like it.

John: We could play some board games or watch a movie.

Jessica: And maybe we can make some cookies! Okay, today is starting to sound better.

John: I was thinking I could do some work on the computer, too. I have a report due next week.

Jessica: It could be a fun and productive day.

John: I always feel like I can do a lot of work when it's rainy because I am not thinking about the need to be outside.

Jessica: That's a good point.

John: Where shall we start?

Jessica: With making cookies, of course!

break the ice: an idiom that means a way to start having a conversation with someone or a group of people you don't know very well. Example: To break the ice, the teacher started class with a fun activity.

controversial: causing people to disagree or argue. Example: Politics can be very controversial.

variety: a number of different things, such as different types of weather. Example: There is a variety of fruit at the grocery store.

seasons: a period characterized by a certain kind of weather; there are four seasons in the year: winter, spring, summer, and fall. Example: My favorite seasons are spring and summer.

forecast: a prediction. Example: The forecast for tomorrow is sunny and 60 degrees.

meteorologist: a person with a science education who is an expert in weather; meteorologists may also tell you the weather forecast. Example: The meteorologist is not always correct.

drought: when there has not been a lot of rain for some time. Example: If there is a drought, you might not be allowed to wash your car with a hose at your house.

rainy season: time of year when most of an area's rain falls. Example: During rainy season you should carry an umbrella.

productive: getting a lot of work done or completing things you need to do. Example: He was very productive today at home and got all of his chores done.

WRITE IT DOWN

What did you do on the last rainy day you can remember? Were you productive? What are some of the advantages of rain? Try using some of the vocabulary you just learned in your explanation.

_____

_____

_____

_____

_____

_____

_____

_____

_____

_____

(Answers will vary.)

Types of Storms

There are many storm types that can happen throughout the year. According to the National Storm Damage Center, some of them include **thunderstorms, ice storms, snowstorms, hail storms, tornadoes, tropical storms,** and **hurricanes**. It is important to listen to the news and follow the advice given when a storm is coming; if we don't, we could be seriously hurt. Out of the storms listed, you might think that snowstorms are the least damaging, but if you try to drive in one, you will soon realize that the chances of crashing your car become much greater than if you were driving in nice weather. Very heavy snowstorms can also cause **power outages**, and sometimes roofs fall down or collapse. You might also think that thunderstorms are not so bad. However, with a thunderstorm comes lightning. Have you heard the saying, "When thunder roars, go indoors"? That is because many times people are playing outside when they hear thunder, but unfortunately, they do not go inside before lightning hits. If lightning hits you, the chances of your living to tell the story are not great. Ideally, when any type of storm comes to your neighborhood, you should try to stay indoors.

TRUE OR FALSE

Let's see how much you may already know about the types of storms that exist by completing this true or false activity. Then, confirm your answers by reviewing the vocabulary list that follows.

_____ **1.** An ice storm does not create freezing rain.

_____ **2.** Hail is rain that is falling in the form of ice balls.

_____ **3.** During a thunderstorm, lightning can strike trees.

_____ **4.** A tropical storm happens when strong winds form over tropical oceans.

_____ **5.** Snowstorms occur when lots of snow falls.

_____ **6.** Tornadoes look like funnels or cones with the wind going in circles.

_____ **7.** A hurricane happens in the tropics when the winds are at 20 miles per hour.

(Answers are on page 250.)

thunderstorms: storms with thunder, lightning, rain, and sometimes hail. Example: Thunderstorms are expected this afternoon, so soccer practice is canceled.

ice storm: freezing rain that sticks to surfaces, making a coat of ice that looks like a glaze. Example: Washington, D.C. had an ice storm that left people without electricity for days.

snowstorm: heavy snow usually accompanied by high winds. Example: The snowstorm was so bad that you could not drive.

hail storms: ice balls that fall from the sky like rain; hail is usually pea-sized but can be as big as a softball. Example: They had hail storms last week that damaged cars.

tornado: very high winds that look like a funnel or cone shape. Example: Some people like to chase tornadoes, but that is not very safe.

hurricane: a storm with high winds; a tropical cyclone with winds of at least 74 miles per hour. Example: Hurricanes are a concern every year in Florida.

tropical storm: a powerful storm that is not as strong as a hurricane. Example: It is better to get a tropical storm than a hurricane.

power outage: when your electric power is not working, many times because an electric line has been knocked down as a result of a storm. Example: She had a power outage at her house last night because of the storm.

STORY TIME

THE BLIZZARD

Last year, Nikhil and Andrew experienced quite a blizzard. Over three feet of snow fell on the ground. They thought they could help each other shovel the snow to make it easier. The plan was to try to shovel every few hours on their own, and then the next day they would go to each other's houses to finish shoveling all of the snow. They ended up shoveling for hours, yet when they woke up, there was probably another two feet of snow. They had not thought about the fact that the strong wind was bringing a lot of snow right back to where they had just shoveled. They couldn't see it because the snow was blowing everywhere. They took a break

from all the shoveling by enjoying some hot chocolate and playing some video games. Fortunately, it stopped snowing by the second day, so they were able to finish shoveling all of the snow. When they were done, they remembered to put salt down on the driveway, which was helpful. They were glad it was over and felt lucky that they did not have a power outage.

1. What is a blizzard?

   A. A heavy snowstorm with winds that make it hard to see

   B. A snowstorm with winds

   C. A snowstorm

2. Why did Nikhil and Andrew put salt on the driveway?

   A. Salt helps you walk in the snow.

   B. Salt helps melt the snow.

   C. Salt is the only thing they sell to put on the driveway for snow.

3. Why were they exhausted?

   A. They had been playing in the snow.

   B. They had been driving for a long time in the snow.

   C. They had been shoveling for a long time.

4. Was it a bad day for them overall?

   A. Yes, they were so tired.

   B. No, they had some fun even though they worked hard.

   C. I can't tell based on what they said in the story.

(Answers are on page 250.)

Have you been in a snowstorm? What steps did you take to prepare for it? Tell us about it here, and then share your story with a friend. (If you have not been in a snowstorm, tell us about another type of storm you have experienced.) Use at least two vocabulary words and one idiom from this or previous chapters.

_____

_____

_____

_____

_____

(Answers will vary.)

Idioms Related to the Weather

Idioms about weather can be quite amusing to learn and use since people always talk about the weather. Look at the following idioms, and circle the ones that you have not heard of before.

raining cats and dogs	when it is raining very heavily
under the weather	when you are not feeling well
fair-weather friend	someone who is only your friend during the good times
a warm welcome	making someone feel included when they first arrive somewhere
weather the storm	to be all right despite some troubling times
calm before the storm	when things seem like they are okay, but you know they are going to get worse
when it rains, it pours	when bad things happen, they seem to happen all at once
steal my thunder	when someone else is getting the attention you thought you would get
take a rain check	when you say you can do something, but only later on (not at the present time)
on cloud nine	when you are very happy

Fill in the blanks with the most appropriate idioms.

1. Her dog died, her mother was sick, and she had a ton of work due the next day. When it _____ , it pours.

2. She was under the _____ and thought she had the flu.

3. Let's give our new friend, Annie, a _____ welcome by taking her out to eat.

4. I think I am going to weather the _____ and keep my job, even though there is a new boss who seems mean.

5. I figured it was the _____ before the storm because he was about to get the bad news.

6. She was on _____ nine after going on that date.

7. It is pouring rain. It is raining cats and _____ .

8. As soon as he started having problems, his _____-weather friends left.

9. If you take a rain _____ , it means you want to do something, just not at that very moment.

10. He came to steal my _____ because he knew I was trying to sell my idea first.

(Answers are on page 250.)

Dealing with Winter Weather and Seasonal Affective Disorder

Seasonal Affective Disorder, also known as SAD, happens to many people in the winter. It means they actually feel sad and get depressed because of the weather and lack of light. People usually begin to get sad when it starts to get cooler around the fall, and they stay sad through the winter months. People with SAD can get treated with light therapy, psychotherapy, or medications. Symptoms include feeling cranky, being very sensitive to other people's comments, sleeping too much, wanting more food with carbohydrates, and gaining weight. If you feel like this during the winter months, you should talk to your doctor. And, if you feel like this all year long, it could still be SAD, or it might be major depression. Either way, talking to your doctor about how you are feeling is a good idea.

light therapy: sitting under or by a special light for a certain amount of time to help with depression. Example: Every winter she uses light therapy.

psychotherapy: when people who are depressed talk to a mental health professional to figure out why they are depressed and learn how they can treat their depression. Example: Psychotherapy can help some people better than others.

symptoms: something that shows you have a certain problem. Example: Keiko's symptoms of depression were feeling tired and having no enthusiasm to do anything.

cranky: feeling irritable or in a bad mood. Example: Leo is always cranky when he has too much work to do.

John and Jessica both felt a bit depressed last year around the time the blizzard hit. Let's see what they were thinking and how they dealt with it in this dialogue.

Jessica: I always feel so tired in winter. I'd rather take a rain check on going places because I just want to get under the covers and sleep.

John: I know what you mean. It's always so dark that it seems like a perfect time to sleep. And I notice that I feel cranky because I have to go to school instead of staying in bed like I want to.

Jessica: I don't feel myself getting cranky, but I do want to eat a lot more sweets.

John: Do you like having hot chocolate and cookies in the winter?

Jessica: They make me feel like I'm on cloud nine, but then I just want to go back to bed. It's especially hard when it gets dark around 5 p.m.

John: By 8 or 9 p.m. it seems like midnight.

Jessica: It's really weird how that works.

How many idioms were in the dialogue? _____

(Answer is on page 250.)

WRITE IT DOWN

We have just been talking about storms and how weather can make you feel sad. Beautiful days can make you feel very good, though. Do you remember feeling great because of the weather? What did you do and why? Tell us about it here, making sure not to leave out any details.

_____

_____

_____

_____

_____

(Answers will vary.)

Vocabulary Crossword

Complete the crossword below using the vocabulary you just learned.

ACROSS

4. I like to watch the Weather Channel and see the _____ tell me the forecast.

5. She would like to try _____ therapy next time it is dark for several days in a row.

6. The first time I saw an _____ storm I thought it looked amazing how everything has glaze on it.

8. They say when _____ roars you should go indoors.

10. There are four _____ in the year.

DOWN

1. She was showing signs or _____ of SAD.

2. It hasn't rained in such a long time. Is there a _____?

3. He was thinking that he wanted to start with _____ the next time he feels depressed so that he can talk about it.

7. During _____ season it seems like it rains every day for months.

9. When _____ storms have very big ice balls or they fall hard they can cause a lot of damage to cars and homes.

(Answers are on page 250.)

Chapter Reflection

The following is a summary of what was covered in this chapter, from talking about the weather to storm types to SAD. You may or may not have experienced all of the types of weather you read about in this chapter, but you now have the vocabulary to discuss them, along with some fun idioms to use in conversations.

Vocabulary

controversial	productive	tropical storm
variety	thunderstorms	power outage
season	ice storm	light therapy
forecast	snowstorm	psychotherapy
meteorologist	hail storms	symptoms
drought	tornado	cranky
rainy season	hurricane	

Idioms

break the ice

raining cats and dogs

under the weather

fair-weather friend

a warm welcome

weather the storm

calm before the storm

when it rains, it pours

steal my thunder

take a rain check

on cloud nine

Do you remember all of the information covered in this chapter? It not, go back and review it to make sure you do. Practice the vocabulary and idioms in your conversations, and look for them when you are reading different materials. Check out the weather forecast on the Weather Channel or online so you can talk about it with people you meet today. Also, look at the weather around the world so that you can compare it to the weather in your area.

CHAPTER 13

Holidays

After reading this chapter, you should know more about . . .

- **Types of holidays**
- **Traditions for holidays**
- **Vocabulary related to holidays, such as the following:**
    - Memorial Day
    - Independence Day
    - Valentine's Day

Holidays in the United States

People in the United States love their holidays. It is a time for family and friends to come together and celebrate. There are several holidays throughout the year, such as **federal holidays**, **state holidays**, **religious holidays**, and **observance days**. In this chapter, we will focus on some of the holidays when many people have a day off from work or take time off to get together and enjoy each other's company. They are spread out throughout the year, as you can see here:

- January—New Year's Day
- February—Valentine's Day
- March—St. Patrick's Day
- May—Memorial Day
- July—Fourth of July/Independence Day
- September—Labor Day
- October—Halloween
- November—Thanksgiving
- December—Chanukah, Christmas, New Year's Eve

DIALOGUE 1

People have favorite holidays, too. Let's see what John and Jessica pick as their favorites in the following dialogue.

John: Thanksgiving is my favorite holiday because you get to eat a lot of turkey.

Jessica: I love turkey, but the sweet potatoes are so delicious. It's like having dessert with dinner.

John: Having the mashed potatoes, rolls, gravy, green beans, cranberry sauce, and all of the other goodies is such a treat. Plus, there's football to watch after you eat all the food.

Jessica: Well, I'm not really into sports, but I can see why you'd like that. I think my favorite holiday is New Year's Eve. There might not be as much food, but it's always exciting getting to

wait to see the ball drop in New York when it's midnight and the New Year begins.

John: I agree. That's a fun one because you can dance all night long.

Jessica: Holidays when we have days off from school are definitely the best, like Memorial Day, Presidents' Day, and Labor Day. I like going to my friends' barbecues on those days.

John: You're making me hungry talking about all this food.

Jessica: Ha ha, let's go eat, then!

federal holidays: days that the government has made official holidays by law, and as a result, the federal government closes on those days. Example: He works at the department store, so he does not get the day off on federal holidays.

state holidays: days selected by a state as holidays, but may or may not be holidays in other states. Example: Patriots' Day is a state holiday in Massachusetts that takes place in April.

religious holidays: days that people from a certain religion observe as holidays. Example: People who observe a religion usually have religious holidays.

observance days: days that are used to remind ourselves of a person, an important cause, or an important celebration, such as Chinese New Year in February, Read Across America Day in March, and Earth Day in April. Example: Observance days provide people time to remember important causes.

WRITE IT DOWN

Do you have a favorite holiday? How does it compare to Thanksgiving? Write about the similarities and differences here, and then talk to a friend to see what his or her favorite holiday is and why that is.

_____

_____

_____

_____

_____

_____

_____

_____

_____

_____

(Answers will vary.)

Valentine's Day

Valentine's Day is a **romantic** holiday that you celebrate with your partner (if you have one). People give each other cards, flowers, and candy; go out to eat; or might even celebrate by going on a short trip. It can be a very happy occasion. **Cupid** is typically seen in stores with his bow and arrow, ready to help two people make a match. Valentine's Day is probably **overrated**, though. Some people think it was created to make people buy things for their loved ones. They think that it is just one day to be extra caring to your partner, and that if you have a partner, you should appreciate them every day. **Regardless**, it is a good day to enjoy sharing with your partner or finding a partner (if you want one). Or, you could get together with your single friends if you don't have a partner and have some fun together! Some people call it "Galentine's Day" for gals celebrating together.

romantic: showing your love or expressing your love to someone. Example: He is very romantic and always buys flowers on their anniversary.

Cupid: the Roman god of love, which usually is shown as a naked figure with wings and a bow and arrow. Example: Cupid appears on many Valentine's Day decorations sold in stores.

overrated: when something is valued or praised too highly. Example: Valentine's Day can be overrated.

regardless: despite everything. Example: She wanted to go out regardless of the fact that her friend didn't want to go.

TRUE OR FALSE

Read the following statements, and write TRUE or FALSE on the line to see how much you know about the holidays we will be talking about next, which are Memorial Day, Labor Day, and the Fourth of July.

_____ **1.** Memorial Day is a day to think about the people who died for the United States.

_____ **2.** Memorial Day used to be called Decoration Day.

_____ **3.** The first state to have Memorial Day as a holiday was Maryland.

_____ **4.** Labor Day is a day to honor people's hard work.

_____ **5.** Labor Day is celebrated in December.

_____ **6.** Labor Day is a federal holiday.

_____ **7.** The Fourth of July is celebrated without fireworks.

_____ **8.** The Fourth of July is also known as Independence Day.

_____ **9.** The Declaration of Independence is celebrated on the Fourth of July.

_____ **10.** There are many sales at stores during Memorial Day, Labor Day, and the Fourth of July.

(Answers are on page 250.)

Match the following words to their definitions using the vocabulary you just learned.

A. Cupid
B. Federal holidays
C. State holidays
D. Romantic
E. Overrated
F. Religious holidays
G. Regardless
H. Observance days

1. _____ days that the government has made official holidays by law, and as a result, the federal government closes on those days

2. _____ days that people from a certain religion observe as holidays

3. _____ the Roman god of love, which usually is shown as a naked figure with wings and a bow and arrow

4. _____ when something is valued or praised too highly

5. _____ days selected by a state as holidays, but they may or may not be holidays in other states

6. _____ despite everything

7. _____ showing your love or expressing your love to someone

8. _____ days that are used to remind ourselves of a person, an important cause, or an important celebration, such as Chinese New Year in February, Read Across America Day in March, and Earth Day in April

(Answers are on page 250.)

Memorial Day, Labor Day, and the Fourth of July

Memorial Day, Labor Day, and the Fourth of July are federal holidays. If you happen to work for the government, you get the day off. Yet, many companies and businesses close for these major holidays, too. Even though they are celebrations for different purposes, people tend to celebrate them in similar ways. For example, many times people have a barbecue with hamburgers and hot dogs on these holidays. They might also have chicken and ribs. Sometimes there are large **firework** displays at night, especially on the Fourth of July. People also buy fireworks to shoot them off on their own. It is not legal in some states to have fireworks, so it is not a good idea to buy them when you are in one state where they are legal and then use them in the state you live in if it's not legal. If you want to buy them, you should make sure what you buy is legal in your state so that you do not get in trouble and have to pay a large **fine**. Interestingly, people get so involved in the planning of the celebrations that they forget what these holidays are about. As mentioned before, Memorial Day is meant to remember the people who have died while serving in the United States' armed forces; Labor Day honors the work that people do in the United States; and the Fourth of July celebrates the country's independence. Next time one of these holidays comes around, ask people what each holiday celebrates to see if they know.

fireworks: explosions of light in the sky made by gunpowder and other chemicals, used to celebrate holidays. Example: I love to see the firework displays on the Fourth of July.

fine: money someone has to pay for doing something wrong. Example: You should not park illegally if you want to avoid a fine.

Idioms Related to Holidays

kick back	to relax
put someone up	to let someone sleep the night; it could be during a holiday or while they find a place to live
holiday spirit	feeling hopeful, cheerful, and positive during the holiday season
feeling stuffed	eating so much that you feel very full
hustle and bustle	busy time with lots of energy and excitement
beat the heat	try to stay inside when it is very hot
recharge your batteries	try to relax and rest to gain your energy back
there's no place like home	home is the best of all places
home is where the heart is	home is where you feel loved and cared for

Idiom Crossword

Complete the crossword below using the idioms you just learned.

ACROSS

2. She is coming for the Fourth of July weekend, so I am going to put her ____.

5. I really need to recharge my ____ so that I am ready to do that big project.

7. I can't wait to ____ back and do nothing.

8. It is nice to visit my family during the holidays because there is no place like home.

9. During the Fourth of July, it is hard to ____ the heat, especially if you live in the southern part of the United States.

DOWN

1. During the holidays there is a lot of ____ and bustle in the grocery store.

3. She was feeling ____ after the Thanksgiving meal.

4. I love to travel, but home is where the ____ is.

6. I could feel their holiday ____ when they were singing songs at the mall.

(Answers are on page 250.)

THANKSGIVING SHOPPING

Jessica wanted to go shopping during Black Friday, *which usually starts at the end of Thanksgiving. She planned to go to sleep early that night and wake up at 2 a.m. to get in line at a store that opened at 3 a.m. She wanted to get a new laptop computer and saw they had a great sale price. They had* marked down *the computer she wanted by almost 50 percent. She would have to convince John to get up and come along because he was convinced that* Cyber Monday *would have better deals. He was also tired after eating a huge meal. In addition, he did not want to deal with the crowds and people fighting over the sale items. He reminded Jessica that last year someone was* trampled *at a store because people just walked on top of them while trying to get into the store. Jessica was not going to* back down *easily. She told John that she didn't think she would find such a good deal if she waited. John then got up, looked online where Cyber Monday deals were listed, and found the computer she wanted on sale. He sent her the link, and she was enthusiastic that it was an even better deal than the Black Friday deal. She went to sleep and thought to herself,* good things come to those who wait.

1. Black Friday is a day for:

    A. Eating leftovers

    B. Shopping

    C. A vacation

2. If the computer was marked down, it meant that it was:

    A. Put on a lower shelf so people could reach it

    B. Last year's model

    C. Selling at a lower price

3. Cyber Monday takes place:

    A. On the Monday after Thanksgiving

    B. Online

    C. Both of the above

4. The person was trampled on Black Friday because:

    A. People were running into the store

    B. The person was very small

    C. The person was sitting on the floor

5. What does *back down* mean in this story?

    A. Disappoint

    B. Apologize

    C. Decide not to go

(Answers are on page 250.)

Black Friday: traditionally the day after Thanksgiving; many stores have sales to get people to shop. Example: I don't like to go shopping on Black Friday because it gets very crowded.

marked down: when something is on sale or at a cheaper price than usual. Example: She bought the jeans because they were marked down.

Cyber Monday: the Monday after Thanksgiving, when there are many online deals to get people to shop online. Example: Shopping on Cyber Monday is a good idea.

trampled: run over. Example: She didn't want to get trampled by the crowds.

back down: decide not to do something. Example: He will not back down once he has made up his mind.

good things come to those who wait: an idiom that means something good will happen if you are patient. Example: It is important to be easygoing because good things come to those who wait.

Have you gone shopping when there was quite a bit of hustle and bustle? There could be some good and bad things about that. Share a story about one of those times, including the good and bad things that happened, and then compare it with a friend's story.

_____

_____

_____

_____

_____

(Answers will vary.)

New Year's Eve

At the end of the year, people come together to celebrate the new year that is coming. They have parties with food and music, play games, and watch television shows that count down to midnight. Sometimes people watch the excitement in Times Square in New York, where they have a ball that drops at midnight. More recently, in Miami, Florida, they have started a tradition where a large orange is lit up and goes up to the top of a building to mark midnight. Once it is midnight, people hug and kiss each other and also call or text friends to say "Happy New Year!" People often make **New Year's resolutions**.

DIALOGUE 2

Let's see what kind of New Year's resolutions John and Jessica made in this dialogue.

Jessica: This year I'm going to start exercising.

John: We say that every year.

Jessica: So maybe we should try eating healthy this time?

John: No, we should try exercising again. The problem is sticking with it.

Jessica: Last year the gym was full of people in January.

John: That's probably because they relaxed and ate too much over the holidays. There's no place like home to get all of your favorite foods.

Jessica: Well, you do have to kick back sometimes.

John: That's true. I have heard it's healthy to let yourself relax once in a while.

Jessica: That's great news!

Look back through the dialogue. How many idioms were used from this chapter? _____

(Answer is on page 250.)

Chapter Reflection

The following is a summary of what was covered in this chapter, from various types of holidays to the traditions that come with them. Many ideas were discussed, so hopefully you feel like you know more about holiday customs in the United States. Are they the same as or different from your holidays? Create a chart showing how similar or different they are to each other.

Vocabulary

federal holidays	overrated	Cyber Monday
state holidays	regardless	trampled
religious holidays	fireworks	back down
observance days	fine	New Year's resolutions
romantic	Black Friday	
Cupid	marked down	

Idioms

kick back	beat the heat
put someone up	recharge your batteries
holiday spirit	there's no place like home
feeling stuffed	good things come to those who wait
hustle and bustle	home is where the heart is

Do you remember all of the information covered in this chapter? If not, go back and review it to make sure you do. Practice the vocabulary and idioms in your conversations, and look for them when you are reading different materials. Make sure to ask someone for more details about the reasons we have certain holidays, and see how much you can add to what you just learned.

Get access to the downloadable audio dialogues for
English USA Every Day at:

http://barronsbooks.com/media/eue2175/

PART TWO

BEING SOCIAL

CHAPTER 14

Discovering Things to Do

After reading this chapter, you should know more about . . .

- **Finding places of interest to visit:**
    - Online
    - At the public library
- **Getting there using a(n):**
    - Bus
    - Taxi
    - Uber
    - Car
- **Using vocabulary for touring the area, such as the following:**
    - Ratings
    - Trip Advisor
    - Guidebook
    - Visuals

Where Can You Find Places of Interest?

It is exciting to learn about a new town. There are so many new things to do, places to go, and people to meet. What places might you want to go to first? Jeff decides to ask Debbie, his favorite barista in his new town, to see what she recommends. See the following dialogue about finding something to do. You can listen to the audio online, too.

DIALOGUE 1

Jeff: Hi, Debbie. Can I get a caramel macchiato? I'm also hoping you can help me with something else. I'm fairly new to the area and am wondering if you could recommend some things to do for fun.

Debbie: Of course! There is a beautiful park called Balboa Park. If you go down this street for about three miles, it'll be on your right. I love having picnics there.

Jeff: That sounds great! Any other ideas?

Debbie: Well, there's La Jolla beach. That's a little farther away, but it's my favorite. You can watch sea lions there!

Jeff: Cool, thanks!

Debbie: If you really want more information about things to do, I'd go to the library if I were you. The librarians can show you books about our area.

Jeff: I'll have to try that!

Debbie: Oh, last thing—the visitor's center is probably another good place to find out about the area. You can look online for its address. I don't remember exactly where it is—I've lived here forever so I never had to go there! Oh, here's your coffee!

---

wondering: wanting to know something. Example: She was wondering when would be a good time to go to the museum.

recommend: to suggest that someone or something would be good or suitable for a particular job or purpose—for example, recommending a specific place to visit that you might like. Example: Can you recommend a place to eat near the theater?

mile: unit of distance, about 1,609 meters. Example: Erika lives about a mile away from the center of town.

sea lion: a large seal that lives in the Pacific Ocean. Example: A sea lion loves to eat fish.

visitor's center: a place where you can get information about a particular area. Example: James always stops at the visitor's center when he gets to a new city.

Based on this dialogue, where would you go to find out about things to do? Tell us here and then make a list of places you would be interested in seeing in San Diego. If you are not sure, do a Google search!

(Answers will vary.)

It is also helpful to look for **ratings** for a location to see what other people have thought of a particular area. Websites such as **Trip Advisor** provide ratings from people who have visited a particular place. It has pictures showing you what the place looks like and provides the website link for the location if it has one. On Trip Advisor, if you type in the name of a city and state, a **drop-down menu** will provide an overview, hotels, vacation rentals, things to do, restaurants, travel guides, and so on. Clicking on "Things to Do" in San Diego, for example, will show you the best-rated places in that city.

Based on Trip Advisor, it appears that the number-one thing to do in San Diego is to visit the USS Midway Museum. A rating of about a 4.5 out of a possible 5 was given by 11,598 people. If you have money to spend, you can click on "More Info" to find out about tours. However, tours are usually expensive and are often not needed. In other words, you can visit many places on your own without a tour.

ratings: reviews about a person, place, or thing. Example: That restaurant got excellent ratings.

drop-down menu: a list that lets you click on what you are interested in learning more about. Example: The Trip Advisor drop-down menu showed me where to find hotels.

Trip Advisor: website that provides ratings from people who have visited a particular place.

Write down the places that you would like to visit in the order you prefer to see them.

_____

_____

_____

_____

_____

(Answers will vary.)

Another great resource is your public library. Librarians can point out a variety of books that talk about your area. The best part is that you can visit the library for free and as often as you like. In a search engine, such as Google, type the city and state followed by the word "library"—for example "San Diego, California library"—to see where all of the libraries in your area are located. The San Diego library has an eCollection of eBooks, eVideos, and eAudiobooks that can be read, seen, or heard online. You will need to have a local identification or driver's license to check out materials. However, even if you don't have one, you can see the materials that are available at the library.

At the library, you can talk to a librarian. They are there to help you. See the following example of a dialogue with a librarian.

DIALOGUE 2

Librarian: Hi, how may I help you?

Jeff: I'm new to San Diego, so I'm looking for guidebooks for the area.

Librarian: Let me look them up on my computer to see where they are located.

Jeff: Thanks.

Librarian: Follow me, and I'll show you where they are located.

Jeff: Is there one that you would rate highly?

Librarian: Oh, yes. I like the *2-3 Travel* books because they have a lot of visuals. Oh, here we are!

Jeff: Thank you very much.

Librarian: You are welcome. Please let me know if I can be of further assistance.

guidebooks: books that tell you about interesting places to visit in a certain area. Example: Jasmine bought guidebooks before going on vacation.

visuals: pictures, drawings, graphs, or tables that help make something easier to understand. Example: Cody likes guidebooks with many visuals.

further assistance: more help. Example: Luca would like further assistance finding a place to stay.

VOCABULARY CHECK

Use the following words in a sentence.

For example:
ratings: *I will be visiting places with high ratings.*

visitor's center: _____

_____

Trip Advisor: _____

_____

drop-down menu: _____

_____

guidebook: _____

_____

visuals: _____

_____

further assistance: _____

_____

(Answers will vary.)

Vocabulary Crossword

Complete the crossword below using the vocabulary you just learned.

ACROSS

3. The website has a drop-down _____ that provides choices to select.
4. The Trip _____ website provides information about places all over the world.
5. The librarian gave further _____ when he asked for more help.
7. The _____ book helped him plan his trip.

DOWN

1. A place with high _____ should be good.
2. He liked that there were many pictures or _____.
6. The visitor's _____ has information about the town.

(Answers are on page 250.)

Interjections

Once you know where you are going, you can figure out how to get there. Do you have a car? Do you need to take a bus? Is there a subway? Are you taking a taxi? Or are you going to take an Uber? You can ask at the local visitor's center for the best way to get around a new city.

See the following example of a dialogue with a visitor's center assistant. Notice the interjections in bold. An interjection is a word or expression that occurs on its own and expresses emotion. They are commonly used in speaking and informal writing, but not much in academic writing. You probably use them all of the time. For example, you might say "Oh?" or "No!" Read the interjections used by Jeff when speaking to Jasmine, the visitor's center assistant, in the following dialogue.

DIALOGUE 3

Jasmine: Hi! How may I help you?

Jeff: What is the best way to get to the San Diego Zoo?

Jasmine: Do you have a car?

Jeff: No, I don't.

Jasmine: Would you like to take a bus, taxi, or Uber?

Jeff: Wow! So many choices! Hmm, let me think about it.

Jasmine: Well, take your time.

Jeff: I'd like to take the bus.

Jasmine: Awesome! Let me show you a map and schedule. If you leave now, you should get there in 45 minutes.

Jeff: Yay! I am happy to hear that! Thanks!

hmm, well: words that show you are thinking about what was just said. Example: Hmm, I am not sure I should go to that party. Well, you should think about it.

wow, awesome, yay: words that show you are excited. (*Wow* could mean you are excited in a positive or negative way. *Awesome* and *yay* mean you are happily excited.) Example: Wow, I am so happy for you! That is awesome! Yay!

MATCHING

The following list of interjections can be used to show your feelings about something. Match each interjection to its correct definition. Some of these interjections mean almost the same thing, so you may match more than one word to the same definition. Please note that some answers may be used more than once.

A. Congrats
B. Bravo
C. Darn
D. Whoops
E. Aww
F. Oh my
G. Oops

1. _____ mistake

2. _____ super performance

3. _____ this is not good

4. _____ something cute or sweet or sad

5. _____ celebrating great news

(Answers are on page 250.)

Write a story about things you might do or places you want to see using many or all of the interjections from the list above. Have fun making it up, and later share it with a friend. Use another sheet of paper if necessary.

_____

_____

_____

_____

_____

(Answers will vary.)

Idioms Related to Traveling

People use idioms or expressions when speaking all the time. Unfortunately, when you translate them word for word, they do not make much sense. Therefore, you just have to learn the meaning of each particular idiom. By learning them, you will be able to understand native English speakers more easily.

in the home stretch	in the last stage of a process
backseat driver	a person in the car who tells you how to drive
miss the boat	miss the opportunity
road rage	when someone driving is angry and drives very aggressively
sail through something	do something with ease
hit the road	depart; begin one's journey
mile a minute	very fast
travel light	bring very few things with you on a trip
off the beaten path	not very well known or popular
all over the place	not well organized
fall into place	when your plans work out nicely
fish out of water	when you feel like you don't belong

Idiom Crossword

Complete the crossword below using the idioms you just learned.

ACROSS

3. He likes to travel _____ so that his suitcase is not heavy.

5. A _____ driver can be annoying.

7. A driver that gets mad might show road _____.

8. Do not _____ the boat. Come with us to the party.

Down

1. You might feel like a _____ out of water at first, but in time you will feel better.

2. He was talking too fast. It seemed like a mile a _____.

4. Everything will fall into _____ because you have planned well.

6. He was able to _____ through something. It was easy for him.

(Answers are on page 250.)

How Will You Get There?

Earlier, you read about how Jeff had choices to get around the town. The person at the visitor's center asked him if he was traveling by car, Uber, bus, or taxi. Jeff was traveling by bus, and fortunately, the person at the visitor's center had a map with the bus routes and times. However, he could have also looked up "San Diego bus schedule" on Google or another search engine.

Let's pretend he took a taxi or Uber instead. He looked up either "San Diego taxi" or "San Diego Uber" on Google to order one. (If he were looking for Uber on a smartphone instead of a computer, he would have downloaded the Uber app to do that.) Once he was in the car with the driver, he had the dialogue on the following page.

Jeff: Hello! You got here quickly.

Driver: Yeah, I was in the area and there was no traffic.

Jeff: Hmm, that's awesome! We'll get to the museum earlier than I thought.

Driver: Aww, is that an accident I see ahead? That's going to impact our arrival time.

Jeff: What? I hope everyone is okay.

Driver: It doesn't look bad. We'll be arriving just a few minutes late, so don't worry.

Jeff: Okay. Are you having a good day?

Driver: Yes, I am. I had several customers today who were very funny. How about you?

Jeff: I will be as soon as I get to the museum. I've wanted to see it for a long time. And when I looked it up on Trip Advisor, it had great ratings.

Driver: My family really likes that museum. Well, we're on the home stretch now. We should be there in just a few minutes.

Jeff: Everything is falling into place today. Thanks!

STOP AND THINK

Did you notice any interjections or idioms in the dialogue? Go back and underline the interjections with one line and the idioms with two lines.

(Answers are on page 251.)

STORY TIME

Read the following story about Jeff's museum visit, and answer the questions that follow.

Jeff arrived at the USS Midway *Museum right on time, and his friend Steve was waiting for him. When Jeff saw him, he gave Steve a hug. They had not seen each other for a while. Once **inside**, they saw many airplanes and ships. In fact, they got to walk **aboard** and **through** some ships. Jeff was delighted because he loves ships. As a young child, he used to make model ships, and he even wanted to become a captain one day. Steve also likes ships, but not as much as Jeff does. He went there more so to see Jeff. Suddenly, they realized the time. It was already 4:00 p.m., and they had not had lunch. "Oh my!" Jeff said. "We should get something to eat." Steve suggested somewhere **across** the street, since museum restaurants tend to be pretty expensive. When they were about to hit the road, they noticed that the museum had an eCollection of eBooks, eVideos, and eAudiobooks. Jeff said, "Yay, this is super! I can spend more time looking at these this weekend."*

1. Why did Steve go to the museum?
    A. To see a highly rated museum
    B. To see the ships and airplanes
    C. To see Jeff
    D. All of the above

2. Jeff was excited about the eCollection because:
    A. He wanted to read more about the museum.
    B. He likes eBooks.
    C. He wanted to show it to his other friends.
    D. He wanted Steve to learn more about ships.

3. What other interjection might Jeff have used instead of "Oh my!"
    A. Wow!
    B. Awesome!
    C. Congrats!
    D. Bravo!

4. Why did they hit the road?
    A. Jeff wanted to get home.
    B. Steve was tired.
    C. They were going to have lunch.
    D. Jeff wanted to fix his car.

5. About when was the last time that Steve saw Jeff?
    A. Yesterday
    B. Last week
    C. A few days ago
    D. A year ago

(Answers are on page 251.)

Chapter Reflection

The following is a summary of what was covered in this chapter, including vocabulary and idioms. We also looked at interjections. Where are you going to go next? Will you visit a museum or go to the library? Discover new things in your own hometown for a fun vacation at home! Think about the tips from this chapter to find your next adventure.

Vocabulary

wondering	guidebook	congrats
sea lion	visuals	bravo
recommend	further assistance	darn
mile	hi	whoops
visitor's center	no	aww
ratings	wow	oh my
Trip Advisor	hmm	oops
drop-down menu	well	aboard
eCollection	awesome	across
eBooks	yay	inside
eAudiobooks	thanks	through

Idioms

in the home stretch	mile a minute
backseat driver	travel light
miss the boat	off the beaten path
road rage	all over the place
sail through something	fall into place
hit the road	fish out of water

Do you remember all of the information covered in this chapter? If not, go back and review it to make sure you do. Practice the vocabulary and idioms in your conversations, and look for them when you are reading different materials. Find an interesting local place to visit on Trip Advisor and take a friend with you!

CHAPTER 15

Travel

After reading this chapter, you should know more about . . .

- **Preparing for a trip**
- **Creating daily plans**
- **Vocabulary related to travel, such as the following:**
    - Itinerary
    - Destination
    - Reservations

Where Will You Go?

Planning a trip can be difficult. Do you want to sit on a beach or explore a national park? Maybe you want to see the sights in Europe. You probably want to think about your budget before deciding on a place to go. If you don't have that much money, a weekend road trip might be in order—that way, you won't miss too much work, don't have to pay for airfare, and will only have to pay for a hotel for a few days. However, if you do have some money saved up for your ideal destination, you can make airline reservations and plan for a longer stay. *Kayak.com* is a good website that can help you find prices for several airlines at one time. It also allows you to conduct other searches at the same time, such as through Priceline, Travelocity, and Expedia, so that you can compare prices. Once you book your flight, the airline will send you your itinerary, which you should print and save or mark in your email so that you can easily find it when you need to check in 24 hours before your flight.

DIALOGUE 1

Bob and Tracey are at a café trying to decide where to go for a long weekend.

Bob: This bagel is a little disappointing. Hey, Tracey, how about we go to New York next weekend? It's supposed to have the best bagels! I heard there's a bus we can take that is pretty cheap.

Tracey: I've heard that the least expensive buses don't guarantee you a seat, though. So, if you don't get there early enough to get a good place in line, you might not get on the bus.

Bob: I guess you get what you pay for, right?

Tracey: I would rather pay a little more and make sure I get a seat.

Bob: We could pack up the car and take a road trip.

Tracey: To where? New York?

Bob: Hey, if you see the waitress let me know. We should get the check. How about we venture up to Canada? Montreal is supposed to be really nice this time of year.

Tracey: Is your passport current? I need to check mine.

Bob: Yes, I'm pretty sure it is. Wouldn't that be fun?

Tracey: I'd like that, especially because we haven't been anywhere for a while. I need a break.

Bob: Or, we could look into flights to California. Have you saved enough for that?

Tracey: How about we figure out how much it will cost to go to Canada first.

Bob: Okay, sounds good to me. Oh, there's the waitress. Check, please!

road trip: going somewhere in your car, such as for a vacation. Example: The family went on a road trip across the country every summer.

airfare: the fee you pay to take an airplane to a certain destination. Example: The airfare for a flight to Miami from New York is about $400 to get there and back. (That is called a roundtrip flight.)

destination: a place you travel to. Example: Her final destination was California, but she had to change planes twice before she got there.

reservations: having something held for you, such as a restaurant or airline saving a seat for you. Example: She made her airline reservations for a trip to Florida three months before she was scheduled to leave.

itinerary: a schedule with travel information. Example: She likes to print out her itinerary so that she does not have to rely on her phone to see it.

venture: to go somewhere that might require courage or that can be dangerous. Example: They wanted to venture out of the city as far as they could.

passport: a document of identification used to show a person's citizenship, allowing a person to travel to different countries. Example: She brought her passport in case they drove into Canada.

TRUE OR FALSE

Let's see how much you know about traveling by answering the following true or false statements.

_____ **1.** The best day to make airline reservations is Tuesday.

_____ **2.** Your destination is the place to which you are going.

_____ **3.** If you venture across the country, you should bring your driver's license or other identification.

_____ **4.** A road trip is always cheaper than flying to your destination.

_____ **5.** You should make your airline reservations a month or more before you travel to get the best deal.

_____ **6.** The itinerary only shows you the time your flight will leave and land.

_____ **7.** You should bring your passport if you are traveling outside of the country.

(Answers are on page 251.)

Preparing for a Trip

If you are going out of the country, make sure your passport is **current** as soon as possible. If it is not, it can take several weeks to **update** or renew it, so you need to plan ahead. It is also a good idea to find out if you will need a **power converter**, **immunizations**, **medicine**, or a **visa**. Looking into the customs of your destination, like if you should take off your shoes when you go in someone's house, can help make sure you have fewer **awkward** moments, too.

Once you have your passport (if you need it) and know how you are getting to your destination, the real fun begins. You can look into cool things to do on Trip Advisor, as mentioned in the previous chapter. This will help you figure out what you should pack. For example, you might need to bring **dressy** clothes, a swimsuit, a sweater, or shorts depending on where you are going. You want to be able to look **dapper** or to **dress down** depending on where you are going, too. **Less is more**, so pack light if you can—that way moving around is easier.

Some other important things to remember include calling your credit card company to let them know you are traveling. You wouldn't want to try and use your card and have it be **declined**. Also, don't forget your cell phone or computer charger and some entertainment for yourself, such as a book or other reading material. These items will help make the time getting there go by faster. Before you know it, you will be at your destination!

current: something that is up to date, such as a passport that has not expired or the latest in pop culture. Example: Sarah always wore the most current fashions when she went out with her friends.

update: to make something current or up to date. Example: He had to update his antivirus software so he wouldn't lose everything on his computer.

power converter: a device that allows you to plug in and charge your electronic devices (cell phone, computer, tablet) into the electric power source in another country, even if the voltage or holes are different from those in your country. Example: Without the power converter, she would not have been able to use her cell phone in Germany.

immunization: an injection to make a person or animal immune to a disease. Example: Before going to Guatemala, you might need a typhoid immunization.

medicine: a treatment used to avoid getting a disease or to help you if you have a disease or other medical condition. Example: She had to take antimalaria medicine during her trip to Rwanda.

visa: mark on a passport allowing a person to enter, stay, or leave another country. Example: She got a visa to go to Tanzania.

awkward: feeling uncomfortable or embarrassed around someone. Example: If you do not study the social customs of the places you visit, you will probably have some awkward moments.

dressy: fancy clothes. Example: He brought his dressy pants because he knew they would be going to a fancy restaurant.

dapper: well dressed and looking good. Example: He looked dapper in his new glasses.

dress down: an idiom that means you wear more casual clothes, such as jeans instead of a suit. Example: In some workplaces, you can dress down on Fridays.

less is more: an idiom that means it can be better to do with less or keep things simple. Example: When you write a letter, less is more if you want to keep your audience engaged.

declined: to be rejected or refused. Example: Her credit card was declined because she forgot to call the bank and let them know she was traveling.

Vocabulary Crossword

Complete the crossword below using the vocabulary you just learned.

ACROSS

3. She packed _____ in case she got sick.

4. Her credit card was _____ because she had not paid her bill.

5. She felt _____ because she only brought shorts, but everyone there wore pants or long dresses.

7. You might not be able to charge your phone in that country without a _____ converter.

9. She needs to make sure her passport is _____.

Down

1. It will take a few weeks to _____ her passport.

2. She needed two _____ before going to Ecuador.

4. She was able to dress _____ when she went to the beach.

6. He was looking very _____ in his suit.

8. She wore her _____ shoes to the party.

(Answers are on page 251.)

Read the following dialogue about some traveling tips Bob and Tracey read online.

Tracey: Hey, Bob, did you make photocopies of your important documents, like your license?

Bob: Yeah, I have copies just in case they are stolen.

Tracey: I still need to do that.

Bob: It's also a good idea to pack your most important things, like medications, in your carry-on since we are flying. I'm so glad you found that great deal on airfare!

Tracey: I was thinking about that. I'll be bringing some ibuprofen, antacids, and other basic things, so I will make sure to put them in my carry-on.

Bob: We should probably keep our money and credit cards in a few different spots in case they get stolen.

Tracey: I hope we don't get robbed. All this talk about having things stolen makes me nervous.

Bob: It's better to be prepared, though.

Tracey: Definitely!

Bob: Last thing—we should probably pack our toiletries in the checked baggage, since airlines don't allow large bottles of liquids. And put them in plastic bags in case they leak!

photocopies: copies made of something, such as your passport, with a copy machine. Example: He made photocopies of his passport before traveling.

carry-on: a small bag that a passenger is allowed to take aboard an airplane. Example: She had to put her purse inside her backpack because the airline only allowed one carry-on.

ibuprofen: a medicine that helps with pain, swelling, and fever. Example: It is amazing how ibuprofen works for so many health issues.

antacid: a medicine that helps lower the amount of acid in your stomach. Example: Every time she eats very spicy foods she needs to take antacids.

toiletries: items for cleaning or grooming yourself, such as shampoo and lotion. Example: She packed too many toiletries, so her luggage was heavy.

checked baggage: the bag(s) that are given to the airline or train crew for them to store in the bottom of the plane or train while you get to your destination. Example: She didn't have many clothes with her because she didn't have any checked baggage. She only brought a carry-on.

WRITE IT DOWN

What might you bring in a carry-on? Look at an airline's website to find out what you can bring before telling us about it here.

_____

_____

_____

_____

_____

(Answers will vary.)

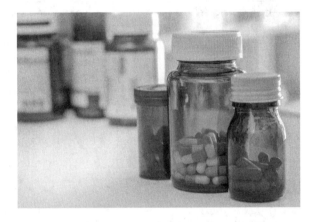

MATCHING

Match the following words to their definitions using the vocabulary you just learned.

A. Carry-on
B. Antacid
C. Ibuprofen
D. Toiletries
E. Photocopies
F. Checked baggage

1. _____ a small bag that a passenger is allowed to take on a plane

2. _____ items for cleaning or grooming yourself, such as shampoo and lotion

3. _____ a medicine that helps lower the amount of acid in your stomach

4. _____ copies made of something, such as your passport, with a copy machine

5. _____ the bag(s) that are given to the airline or train crew for them to store in the bottom of the plane or train while you get to your destination

6. _____ a medicine that helps with pain, swelling, and fever

(Answers are on page 251.)

Idioms Related to Traveling

Which of the following idioms have you heard of? Circle the ones you know.

take for a ride	when you deceive or betray someone
live out of a suitcase	when you travel a lot
go overboard	when you do too much
throw someone under the bus	blame someone for something rather than get in trouble yourself
part ways	stopping a relationship (business or personal), often because of a disagreement
that ship has sailed	an opportunity you missed because it already happened or a situation that is too late to change
on board	when you are in agreement or give your support
move on	to continue progressing or moving
not going to fly	something that will not happen or succeed

STOP AND THINK

Fill in the blanks with the most appropriate idioms you just learned.

1. She really needs to _____ on with her life if she wants to find a new job.

2. He thought he could do it, but that _____ has sailed.

3. He will take you for a _____ if you lend him money.

4. She is on _____ and ready to work with the team.

5. She got tired of traveling for work and living out of a _____ .

6. I don't want to throw anyone under the _____ , but I am not the one who ate all of the cookies.

7. That bad behavior is not going to _____ at school.

8. He will go _____ and try to give you everything you need and more.

9. We need to part _____ and create our own goals.

(Answers are on page 251.)

Creating Daily Plans

Once you know where you are going, having a list of what you want to do each day can help you get the biggest bang for the buck. You can wake up and get right to the museum, park, or wherever you decide to go that day without having to spend time figuring out what you want to do. It will also help you avoid pitfalls, such as getting to a place and finding out it is closed on Mondays, for example. It can also help prevent arguments if you and your traveling companions have agreed to the plans before you go. You would still probably have to decide where to eat, but you might want to ask the locals in the area for recommendations. They might have better advice than a website or app, but, in a pinch, you can always look on Yelp. It is also fun to talk to locals to get a sense of the culture. They might also have tips for places that are a must-see that you can add to your daily plans. Don't forget to have fun!

---

bang for the buck: an idiom that means you get as much as you can for your money. Example: She found some coupons online, so she got the biggest bang for the buck.

pitfall: a problem or danger that might not be obvious. Example: A pitfall of using the low-airfare airline was that they couldn't choose their seats, so they ended up in different rows.

locals: people from a particular area. Example: The locals in Cape Cod were very friendly.

in a pinch: an idiom that means if necessary. Example: She can look that up online in a pinch.

must-see: something that is really worth seeing. Example: The Grand Canyon is a must-see landmark.

DIALOGUE 3

Read the next dialogue to find out what Bob and Tracey decided to do on their trip. They are at the airport getting ready to board.

Tracey: I'm so happy we decided to go to the Grand Canyon!

Bob: I think it was a good idea to travel within the United States because there is so much we have not seen.

Tracey: The Grand Canyon is a must-see. Woohoo!

Bob: It was a great idea to look for Skywalk coupons, because that can be pretty expensive, I hear.

Tracey: That is going to be really interesting— walking on clear glass over the canyon. Kind of scary!

Bob: It got great reviews online.

Tracey: I hope the locals can give us good lunch recommendations!

Bob: Yes, and it will be nice to be out hiking, too.

Tracey: We should look into riding a donkey down the canyon. When in Rome, you know?

Bob: Let's do it! When is the next time we would be going there? Probably not for a very long time, if ever again. We should take advantage and do as much as we can. Maybe we can do some river rafting?

Tracey: I'm on board with that. Speaking of boarding, they just called our flight. It's time to go!

woohoo: a word used to show you are excited. Example: I just won a free airline ticket. Woohoo!

hiking: walking a long distance—for example, on a trail or in the woods. Example: They went hiking on some trails by the waterfall.

when in Rome (do as the Romans do): an idiom that means that you should act like or do the things that the locals would do. Example: He wanted to try some of the local fry bread and thought to himself, when in Rome . . .

WRITE IT DOWN

What else do you think Bob and Tracey should do while on their vacation? If you were to go to the Grand Canyon, what would you want to do? Look at the Grand Canyon National Park website at *https://www.nps.gov/grca/index.htm* to find out more about it.

_____

_____

_____

_____

_____

_____

(Answers will vary.)

STORY TIME

AT THE GRAND CANYON

Tracey and Bob thought they were well prepared for their vacation. They had purchased their airline tickets in advance for the best deal, packed the right clothes, had the necessary toiletries, and made daily plans. What they forgot to plan for was losing their luggage. Tracey's bag was nowhere to be found when they arrived at their destination. As much as she liked shopping for clothes, she was hoping the

airline would find her bag. They told her that they could bring it to her hotel when they found it. She did not get it until the next day, so she had to get a new toothbrush and underwear, but at least she did not have to buy anything else. She thought that in the future she would pack those in her carry-on just in case. It was a lesson learned. The rest of their trip went smoothly. Everything worked out just as they wanted, and they had the best time of their lives.

1. What is an example of a toiletry?

   A. Toilet paper

   B. Pens

   C. Shampoo

2. Why did they buy their airline tickets in advance?

   A. To get a good price

   B. So they could make their daily plans

   C. To show their friends

3. Why didn't they plan for losing their luggage?

   A. They didn't know it could get lost.

   B. They forgot.

   C. They wanted to keep their luggage.

4. Did the airline find her bag?

   A. Yes

   B. No

5. What was the lesson learned?

   A. They needed to plan more carefully.

   B. Tracey needed to pack some more important items in her carry-on.

   C. Both of the above

(Answers are on page 251.)

Chapter Reflection

The following is a summary of what was covered in this chapter, including how to prepare for a trip, tips for traveling, and creating daily plans. Hopefully you can travel somewhere soon so that you can try out some of the suggestions.

Vocabulary

road trip	immunization	antacid
airfare	medicine	toiletries
destination	visa	checked baggage
reservations	awkward	pitfall
itinerary	dressy	locals
venture	dapper	must-see
passport	declined	woohoo
current	photocopies	hiking
update	carry-on	
power converter	ibuprofen	

Idioms

dress down	go overboard
less is more	throw someone under the bus
bang for the buck	part ways
in a pinch	that ship has sailed
when in Rome (do as the Romans do)	on board
take for a ride	move on
live out of a suitcase	not going to fly

Do you remember all of the information covered in this chapter? If not, go back and review it to make sure you do. Practice vocabulary and idioms in your conversations, and look for them when reading different materials. Next time you travel, don't forget to look back at this chapter so you can be prepared for a great time! What must-see place will you go to next? Do some research and plan ahead.

CHAPTER 16

Meeting New People

After reading this chapter, you should know more about . . .

- **Places to go**

- **Meeting people online**

- **Vocabulary related to meeting people, such as the following:**

    - Gathering

    - Assemblage

    - Organization

Volunteering

People are very busy these days, so it can be hard to meet new people at work. However, there are some good ways to meet people outside of work. For example, find out where you can **volunteer**. If you visit *allforgood.org*, you can find many **opportunities** to do so, from adult education to working in the environment to teaching technology. There are many other ideas, too. If you look at the adult education section on the All for Good website, you will find out that you can help with things such as library events, hosting a family, or helping people by using **therapy dogs**. If you **research** the environmental **opportunities**, you will see that various **organizations** can use **landscaping** and **assistance** with their nature centers. Or, if you click on technology, you will find that you can help with **videography**, web pages, and technical support, among many other possibilities.

DIALOGUE 1

Juan and Sofia are out for a bike ride and are trying to figure out where to volunteer.

Sofia: I'm so glad we're sticking with our resolution to exercise. Now I need to work on my other resolution—volunteering! I'm going to look into volunteer opportunities that help **immigrants**. Do you want to join me?

Juan: What would I need to do?

Sofia: I'm not exactly sure. The ad says that we would give parents support to meet their learning goals. It doesn't say much more.

Juan: Do you think we might help them learn English?

Sofia: That's what I am thinking. It should be fun helping them practice.

Juan: Yeah, that might be fun and rewarding for us because we could help them out just like people have helped us.

Sofia: That's one of the reasons I picked this group. There were so many to choose from, but this one sounded interesting and made me feel like I could **pay it forward**.

Juan: I hope the hours are on the weekends.

Sofia: Well, let's call and find out the details.

Juan: Okay, sounds like a plan. Race you to the park entrance!

Sofia: You're on!

volunteer: working or helping to do something without getting paid. Example: When people volunteer they should take it seriously and show up on time.

therapy dogs: dogs that are trained to be friendly and provide comfort to people in hospitals, schools, or other places. Example: She raises therapy dogs for children with autism.

research: getting information about something. Example: He is going to research ways to meet new people.

opportunities: possibilities, or the chance to get something, such as a volunteer position or a job. Example: Carissa is looking into different opportunities to get experience in a hospital.

organization: a group of people who work together to accomplish the same goals. Example: That organization is working to become larger.

landscaping: making the land look nice by doing things such as cutting the grass, planting trees and flowers, and trimming bushes. Example: Aubrey always does such a great job with the landscaping at her house.

assistance: giving help or support to someone.

Example: Tucker would like to give you assistance to find a new job.

videography: the art of making videos. Example: Olivia's videography skills improved after she took the video editing class.

immigrants: people who move to another country to live there. Example: Kanyarose's parents were immigrants from Thailand.

pay it forward: an idiom that means being kind to someone because someone has been kind to you. Example: Aaron would like to pay it forward and drive you to work today.

WRITE IT DOWN

Would you be interested in volunteering? What kinds of things would you be interested in doing? Look on the All for Good website to find ideas. Tell us about three opportunities and why you are interested in them.

_____

_____

_____

_____

_____

_____

_____

(Answers will vary.)

Fill in the blanks with the most appropriate vocabulary words you just learned.

1. The school's land looked like no one had been taking care of it. It needed a lot of _____ .

2. I could use some help, or _____ , in learning how to meet new people.

3. To find volunteer spots, you could do some online _____ .

4. I found many volunteer _____ on the All for Good website.

5. There are many _____ that have volunteer jobs available.

6. She thought that making videos, or _____ , would be a fun way to volunteer and help out.

7. _____ move to a new country to gain work experience or go to school, or perhaps for another reason.

8. Did you want to _____ your time by working there for free?

9. He wanted to pay it _____ and volunteer to help children learn to read after school.

10. She has a _____ dog that she brings to the hospital on Tuesdays.

(Answers are on page 251.)

Birthday Parties

Adults sometimes have birthday parties when they are turning 30, 40, 50, or 60. There might be a gathering or assemblage of people whom you have not met before at the event. And, even though you might be nervous and want to tell your friend that you are not interested in going to the party, you should not. It could be a great opportunity to meet new people. Ask them what you should bring, such as some snacks, drinks, or a gift. An appropriate gift might be a small item for their home. Asking your friend will help you make sure you don't get embarrassed if everyone else brings something and you don't. Remember, they will likely have food and drinks there, people to meet, and maybe even some games to play.

gathering: an occasion when people come together. Example: There will be a small gathering at my house to celebrate her birthday.

assemblage: a group of people or things. Example: There was an assemblage at the church for the concert.

embarrassed: feeling bad or ashamed about something. Example: He feels embarrassed about getting to your party so late.

Use the following words you just learned in sentences related to this chapter's topic of meeting people. Try to use another vocabulary word from a previous chapter as well.

gathering

_____

assemblage

_____

embarrassed

_____

(Answers will vary.)

Meetups

Have you heard of meetups? A meetup is a group of people who get together because they have similar interests. If you visit *meetup. com,* you will find groups that cook, train for a marathon, practice a language, talk about books, walk, or write—just to name a few of the many activities. You can look for meetup groups that are as close as two miles from you to groups that are 100 miles or more away from where you live. It is especially helpful if you just moved somewhere or just want to try something new and need people to go with you. Sometimes the ideas for the meetups are free, while other times they are not. You just have to do a little research, and you will see that there is something for everyone on *meetup.com.* If you join a group, you can share a little bit about yourself online, along with a picture (if you want) so that people can identify you when you meet up with the group. However, if you would rather not include your name and a picture, that is fine, too. Some people use a picture of a place or a cartoon to represent themselves and give themselves a screen name— that way, you can remain anonymous online, and when you get to the meetup you can decide if you want to stay and join the group or leave.

meetup: a gathering of people with similar interests. Example: You can meet many people in a meetup, such as through *meetup.com.*

represent: speaking for someone or a group. Example: He will be at the meeting to represent the team.

screen name: a name you use online that is not your real name. Example: My screen name is Gigi because I always liked that name.

anonymous: someone who is not named or identified. Example: She would like to be anonymous when she responds to the group online.

Vocabulary Crossword

Complete the crossword below using the vocabulary you just learned.

ACROSS

2. He was looking for a _____ where people go hiking.

4. I would like to go to the _____ at her house to meet people.

6. She wanted to be _____, so she was very careful about what she said about herself online.

7. There will be a large _____ of people at the church on Sunday.

DOWN

1. She used a cartoon of a puppy to _____ herself online.

3. She was _____ because she forgot to bring a gift to the birthday party.

5. He used a _____ name online so that people would not know his real name.

(Answers are on page 251.)

(Answers are on page 251.)

STORY TIME

THE MEETUP EXPERIENCE

Sofia wanted to meet some people interested in walking so she could get a little exercise, so she decided to look into a meetup via meetup.com. She quickly found three different walking groups in her area. She went to the first group and found that the people wanted to walk *extremely* fast. She liked getting the exercise but thought it was quicker than she wanted. She went to the next meetup group and found that the group walked pretty slowly. The people in that group were also several years older than she. Finally, she tried the third group in her area. That group walked at a good *pace*, but the people in it were kind of annoying. They complained about everything. She decided that the best group for her was the first group. Even though they walked very fast, she figured it was a *positive challenge* for her, and the people in the group were very nice. It was perfect after all.

1. Which group did Sofia end up liking the best?

    A. First

    B. Second

    C. Third

2. How often does Sofia go walking?

    A. One time a week

    B. Two times a week

    C. We do not know based on the story.

3. What did it mean when she said it was a good pace?

    A. She liked the people.

    B. It was a good speed.

    C. Neither of the above

4. What is a positive challenge?

    A. Something difficult to do

    B. Something good to do

    C. Something that is difficult to do but makes you feel good to do it

5. Did Sofia succeed in finding the perfect walking group?

    A. Yes

    B. No

    C. It wasn't perfect, but she liked it.

(Answers are on page 251.)

Idioms About Meeting People

Since most people need or want to be around people, there are many idioms about people's interactions or connections. Look at the following idioms, and circle the ones you have not seen before.

meeting of the minds	when people agree or share the same opinions on something
friends in high places	you know people who can help you get something you want
whatever floats your boat	whatever works best for you
build bridges	create a connection with someone
man's best friend	a dog
move in the same circles	people with similar interests or backgrounds socialize with each other and likely know some of the same people
birds of a feather (flock together)	people who are similar are friends
two's company, three's a crowd	when a couple wants to be alone, they don't want a third person around them
cross someone's path	meeting someone by chance, not by choice
speak the same language	people who understand each other because they have the same thoughts or views
on the same page	you understand what a person means and agree with them
rub shoulders	when you get a chance to talk to someone, such as with someone famous
a friend in need is a friend indeed	when someone helps you during the hard times, you know that person is really your friend
meet someone halfway	you negotiate an agreement with someone whereby you both are okay with the end result

Fill in the following blanks using the idioms you just learned.

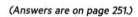

1. She was able to rub _____ and meet the president of the organization.

2. I hope to _____ his path again someday. He was delightful but unfortunately does not live in this area.

3. She went to the meeting to build _____ in hopes of getting a new job.

4. There was a meeting of the _____ , and we agreed on going out to eat.

5. She said, "Whatever floats your _____" when I suggested that we go to the mall.

6. Man's best _____ is a dog.

7. Those three are _____ of a feather. You see them together at every school play.

8. When someone says _____ company, three's a crowd, it is time to leave.

9. I have a friend in _____ places, so hopefully she will be able to get us into that concert for free.

10. We speak the same _____ because we both love comic books.

11. He is a true friend because he helped me move. A friend in need is a friend _____ .

12. If you meet someone _____ , it means that you came to an agreement about something.

13. I was on the same _____ as she was because we both wanted to save our money and find a free meetup.

14. We do not move in the same _____ because she gets to go to events with the president and I do not.

(Answers are on page 251.)

DIALOGUE 2

Let's see how Juan and Sofia use some of the idioms and vocabulary we have learned in the following conversation. People normally don't use this many idioms in a short conversation, but we want you to have fun listening to and looking for them. Underline the idioms and vocabulary you've learned in this chapter.

Sofia: Hey, Juan, do you have any friends in high places that can get us tickets to the concert on Saturday?

Juan: I wish I did. It's supposed to be quite the gathering!

Sofia: I know, and it's sold out.

Juan: Maybe we can sit outside and have a picnic in the parking lot and listen to it.

Sofia: Or, if we can't get tickets, maybe we can volunteer.

Juan: Great idea! Let's do some research and see if that's a possibility.

Sofia: I love when we have a meeting of the minds.

Juan: Which organization is in charge of the concert?

Sofia: I'm embarrassed to say I don't know.

Juan: That's okay. We are birds of a feather. I don't know either!

Sofia: Wish me luck as I try to build bridges and get us a volunteer job.

Juan: Good luck!

How many idioms did you find? _____

How about vocabulary words? _____

(Answers are on page 251.)

Sign Up for a Class

Another way to meet people is to sign up for a class. Not only would you learn something of interest, but you would also get the chance to meet people who are interested in learning the same thing. It is a win-win situation. You could look the classes up online by searching through your local community center, community college, or public library to see what they have that piques your interest. There are classes in which to learn karate, guitar, computer skills, painting, cooking, dancing, another language—you name it!

win-win: good for everyone. Example: If we both get to go to the party, it will be a win-win situation.

piques: excites. Example: She wanted to find out what piques your interest.

you name it: anything you might want. Example: I am open to that or any other idea—you name it!

WRITE IT DOWN

What class might pique your interest? Have you been thinking about it for a while, or is it a new interest? Tell us why you would like to take it, and then share it with a friend. Maybe you could take the class together!

_____

_____

_____

_____

_____

(Answers will vary.)

Chapter Reflection

The following is a summary of what was covered in this chapter. You learned about where to meet people, different websites for meeting people and finding volunteer groups, and idioms about relationships with people.

Vocabulary

volunteer	assistance	meetup
therapy dogs	videography	represent
research	immigrants	screen name
opportunities	gathering	anonymous
organization	assemblage	win-win
landscaping	embarrassed	piques

Idioms

pay it forward	two's company, three's a crowd
meeting of the minds	cross someone's path
friends in high places	speak the same language
whatever floats your boat	on the same page
build bridges	rub shoulders
man's best friend	a friend in need is a friend indeed
move in the same circles	meet someone halfway
birds of a feather (flock together)	you name it

Do you remember all of the information covered in this chapter? If not, go back and review it to make sure you do. Practice vocabulary and idioms in your conversations, and look for them when you are reading different materials. Look at either the Meetup or All for Good websites, and find somewhere to go to meet people this weekend. By meeting new people you will get more opportunities to practice your English skills.

CHAPTER 17

Dating

After reading this chapter, you should know more about . . .

- **Where to meet**

- **Online dating**

- **Vocabulary related to dating, such as the following:**

    - Compatible

    - Significant other

    - Blind date

What to Look for in a Partner

If you are looking for a partner, you probably want someone who is compatible with you because even though some people think that opposites attract, that might not always work in the long run. For that reason, you should consider someone who has at least some similar interests. It is interesting how people sometimes just click. They meet and automatically hit it off. The conversation between them flows naturally, they enjoy listening to each other, and they can easily laugh at each other's jokes. These are some characteristics of a healthy relationship. If you are fortunate to meet someone like that, before you know it you might be calling them your mate, boyfriend, girlfriend, significant other, fiancée, husband, hubby, wife, or wifey.

DIALOGUE 1

Juan and Sofia are heading out to meet their friend's new girlfriend for the first time. Let's see what they think about finding a good partner in this dialogue.

Sofia: I really hope she's a good fit for Carlos. His last girlfriend was no good for him. It's hard to find someone you just click with easily.

Juan: I know what you mean. You meet people who seem nice, but you just know they're not the one for you.

Sofia: You also have to really want a significant other, which I know Carlos does. I'm not sure I'm interested in having a serious relationship right now, though.

Juan: Is that because you haven't found someone compatible with you?

Sofia: I guess that's true. Maybe if I happened to bump into Mr. Right, I would say I'm interested in a serious relationship.

Juan: I hope my Mrs. Right is out there, but, honestly, I'm too busy with school and everything else that I don't have time to even think about that.

Sofia: Well, if you met someone you clicked with and they had values similar to yours, I think you might change your mind.

Juan: I suppose that's true.

Sofia: I also think part of our issue is that we don't go out of our way to meet people since we are not in a rush to have a boyfriend or girlfriend. We just get together with friends!

Juan: Yeah, if I really wanted a girlfriend, I would make more of an effort to find one.

Sofia: There are a lot of ways to meet people online now, so I might try that. It seems like otherwise I just see the same people all the time.

Juan: That's how Carlos met Erica! Maybe you'll have the same luck!

compatible: able to get along. Example: They are not very compatible, so I don't know why they are still together.

in the long run: an idiom that means after a long period of time, or in the future. Example: She would like to meet someone that she can be with in the long run.

click: an idiom that means to connect with someone easily. Example: Sometimes people just click as soon as they meet.

hit it off: an idiom that means to make a connection with someone easily. Example: It was great that they hit it off so well.

characteristics: qualities or features of something or someone. Example: He has many positive characteristics you should consider before making up your mind.

mate/boyfriend/girlfriend/significant other: other ways to refer to your partner. Examples:

- She is currently living with her mate.
- He would like to be more than just a boyfriend.
- She would like to become his girlfriend.
- He has a significant other that no one has ever met.

fiancée: a woman who is engaged to be married.

husband: a man who is married. Example: She met her husband last year at the picnic.

hubby: an informal term for a husband. Example: Her hubby helps her around the house with all of the chores.

wife: a woman who is married. Example: He would like his wife to come to the party with him.

wifey: an informal term for a wife. Example: He affectionately calls his wife "wifey" all the time.

the one: an idiom that means the perfect person for you or the person you are going to marry. Example: Some people do not believe in "the one."

Mr. Right/Mrs. Right: an idiom that also means the perfect person for you/the person you want to marry. Examples:

- Your Mr. Right might be at the party so I hope you go.
- She became Mrs. Right to him when he learned that she likes to watch football.

go out of our way: to inconvenience yourself while doing something that requires a lot of effort. Example: We would go out of our way for you because you are always so helpful.

WRITE IT DOWN

What are the characteristics you look for in a partner? Why? Do you always look for the same things or have you changed what you want recently? List what your ideal partner would be like here, and talk to a friend about it to see what he/she looks for, too. Maybe you can set each other up on a date!

_____

_____

_____

_____

_____

(Answers will vary.)

Match the following words to their definitions using the vocabulary and idioms you just learned.

A. Characteristics
B. Husband
C. Click
D. Hubby
E. Go out of our way
F. Wifey
G. The one
H. Significant other
I. Compatible
J. In the long run

1. _____ able to get along

2. _____ an idiom that means after a long period of time, or in the future

3. _____ an idiom that means to connect with someone easily

4. _____ qualities or features of something or someone

5. _____ an informal term for a husband

6. _____ an informal term for a wife

7. _____ another way to refer to your partner

8. _____ an idiom that means the perfect person for you/the person you want to marry

9. _____ to inconvenience yourself while doing something that requires a lot of effort

10. _____ a man who is married

(Answers are on page 251.)

Red Flags

Just as you want to look for someone who is compatible with you, you also want to look for red flags. Red flags are signs that show you that someone might not be a good match for you (or possibly for anyone). For example, trust is very important in building a relationship. If you start dating someone and find out that they lied to you about something, you  might want to decide not to go out with them again. Another red flag is if they become controlling. If they are upset about you meeting your family and friends or simply doing what you normally do because they want you to be with them at all times, that is another red flag. It is also a good idea to listen to your friends and family about their opinions. If they do not like your new partner, listen to their concerns. It might be a good idea to cut it off before it is too late.

On the way home from meeting Erica, Juan and Sofia talk about how they have dealt with red flags in the past.

Juan: Erica seemed really nice. I didn't get any red flags, did you?

Sofia: None! They seemed to really fit together.

Juan: Do you remember when I went out with Susana? That was a nightmare.

Sofia: Oh, yes! I remember she was a stalker. That was actually pretty creepy.

Juan: It took so long for her to get out of my life. I thought it was never going to end. She would just show up at my house at all times of the day or night.

Sofia: I remember when she would get into arguments with you, I would feel bad for you because she was so disrespectful and would call you names. I couldn't believe you didn't break up with her sooner.

Juan: I tried, believe me. She would apologize and say how much she wanted it to work out.

Sofia: She even got your passwords and looked at your emails and then wanted to spend your money. I couldn't believe it.

Juan: Neither could I. She was so weird. I remember at the beginning of our relationship she would stonewall me whenever I tried to arrange a date.

Sofia: That was annoying, I'm sure, but I think when she started the yelling, that was even more exasperating.

Juan: What about when you went out with that guy Scott? He was nothing to write home about.

Sofia: Oh, that's right. I guess I blocked him from my memory! Sometimes we just want to forget. He was infuriating, too.

Juan: I think we'll be better at spotting red flags in new relationships now.

Sofia: Yeah. I'd want to give someone new a chance, but if they started showing red flags, I would cut them off ASAP.

---

cut it off: to end something, such as ending a relationship. Example: She should cut it off before he becomes worse.

stalker: a person who is obsessed with someone and follows, watches, or bothers that person in a troublesome or frightening way. Example: He met the stalker in a club last month.

creepy: causing you to feel scared or upset. Example: He was very creepy, so she left the party.

stonewall: not answering or talking to someone. Example: When they get into arguments, she will just stonewall him.

exasperating: causing you to feel extremely annoyed or irritated. Example: I find it exasperating how some people behave in public.

nothing to write home about: an idiom that means someone or something that is not that good or not worth sharing information about. Example: Sean met someone at the party, but she was nothing to write home about.

infuriating: making someone very angry. Example: He can be infuriating when he does not have the patience to carefully do his work.

ASAP: an acronym for as soon as possible. Example: He would like to leave this place ASAP.

Mark the following statements about relationships as true or false.

_____ **1.** If someone you just started dating is creepy, you should keep going out with him/her.

_____ **2.** A stalker might follow you to work.

_____ **3.** People who are exasperating are usually very nice.

_____ **4.** If you need to get somewhere ASAP, you'd better hurry up.

_____ **5.** When someone stonewalls you, he or she doesn't talk to you.

_____ **6.** If a relationship is working, you should cut it off.

_____ **7.** If someone is always making you feel good about yourself, it can be infuriating.

_____ **8.** He is nothing to write home about because he did not want to hear about her bad day at work.

(Answers are on page 251.)

Where Can You Find a Partner?

In Chapter 16 we talked about ways to meet people in general by volunteering, going to birthday parties, attending meetups, and signing up for classes. Those are good ways to meet a partner, too; however, you might also consider online dating. There are numerous websites and apps that are commonly used in the United States to meet a new partner, such as Match, OkCupid, Tinder, and eHarmony. To join those websites, you usually have to answer several questions about yourself. This lets other people on the site know about you. If you want to try one out for free, OkCupid is a good place to start. You answer the questions, create your profile with information about yourself—including some pictures—and then you can start looking for a partner. You can select people based on their age, level of school they have completed (high school or bachelor's, master's, or doctorate degree), work, children, and so on. You select the categories that are must-haves, and then the website will show you who fits those criteria. If you look at any of the dating websites or apps, you will see that many people have found partners through them. You just might have to kiss a lot of frogs before finding your prince (or princess), but remember that there are plenty of fish in the sea.

criteria: standards you might have for something or someone.

kiss a lot of frogs before finding your prince: an idiom that means to go out with several people before meeting the right match for you.

there are plenty of fish in the sea: an idiom that means there are many potential mates out there, so you shouldn't worry if you have not found a good partner yet.

Would you use or have you used an online dating website? If you did, how did it go? If you would, why would you? If you would not, why not? Look at a few to see what they offer before answering here.

_____

_____

_____

_____

_____

_____

(Answers will vary.)

Idioms About Dating

Idioms about dating or relationships can be funny. Read over the following idioms, and circle the ones you have not seen before.

match made in heaven	a couple that gets along very well; a partnership that works very well
pop the question	ask someone to marry you
blind date	a date between two people who have never previously met; usually a friend or family member sets up the blind date
go Dutch	when you and your partner split the bill for dinner or the overall date
cheat on	when one partner is not faithful to the other
drool over	when you look at someone and think he or she is very attractive
tie the knot	get married
get stood up	when someone does not show up for your date
make eyes	when you look at someone flirtatiously because you like them
out of your league	someone who you think would not be interested in you
catfishing	pretending to be someone else on social media in order to con someone into an online relationship
third time is the charm	the third time you do something, it finally works out for you

Idiom Crossword

Complete the crossword below using the idioms you just learned.

ACROSS

4. He wanted to tie the _____ but she was not ready.

6. She had two long-term relationships that failed, yet she is determined that the third time will be the _____.

7. You should not _____ over someone just because they are beautiful.

10. They were making _____ throughout the party. I think they like each other.

11. I don't know how long he is waiting to pop the _____.

DOWN

1. They split everything when they go out. They always go _____.

2. She stopped going out with him because he cheated _____ her.

3. She regretted going on the _____ date because he was not compatible.

5. It is not fun when you get _____ up on a date.

6. He thought he found a perfect match, but she was _____ him.

8. She is out of your _____ because she works very hard and you don't want to find a job.

9. It is such a pleasure seeing how well they get along. They are a match made in _____.

(Answers are on page 251.)

(Answers are on page 251.)

STORY TIME

MOVIE: ONLINE DATING SAFETY

Juan started dating someone online. He didn't think he had to worry too much about online dating safety because he was a guy. He quickly found out he was wrong. He had put his cell phone number in his profile, which he later found out was a bad idea. A girl he went out with only one time kept calling him, even though he told her he didn't think they were going to work out. He was careful in that he was watching for red flags, and the fact that she did not listen to his request was a red flag. They say to go with your gut, and his gut was saying she was not right for him. She seemed very needy and obsessive. At least he knew better than to send her money when she started begging for it, saying she was going to get kicked out of her apartment because she couldn't pay the rent. He blocked her number and quickly removed his number from his profile. He also made sure to tell a friend when he was going out with someone new, whom he would always meet in a public place. He figured that by doing so, his friend could try to find him if something went wrong.

1. What mistake did Juan make?

   A. He gave personal information on his profile.

   B. He told the girl they were not a good match.

   C. He was mean to the girl.

2. How many times did he go out with the girl before she started stalking him?

   A. One

   B. Two

   C. Three

3. What does it mean to go with your gut?

   A. Notice how your stomach feels.

   B. Follow your instincts.

   C. Eat when you are hungry.

4. He always meets his dates in

   A. his house.

   B. a restaurant.

   C. public.

5. When dating online, you must be careful

   A. online.

   B. on the date.

   C. online and on the date.

(Answers are on page 251.)

Chapter Reflection

The following is a summary of what was covered in this chapter, including what to look for in a partner, red flags to watch out for, and where to find a potential mate. Most important, being safe when dating is key.

Vocabulary

compatible	fiancée	creepy
characteristics	husband	stonewall
mate	hubby	exasperating
boyfriend	wife	infuriating
girlfriend	wifey	ASAP
significant other	stalker	criteria

Idioms

in the long run	pop the question
click	blind date
hit it off	go Dutch
the one	cheat on
Mr. Right/Mrs. Right	drool over
go out of our way	tie the knot
cut it off	get stood up
nothing to write home about	make eyes
kiss a lot of frogs before finding your	out of your league
prince	catfishing
there are plenty of fish in the sea	third time is the charm
match made in heaven	

Do you remember all of the information covered in this chapter? If not, go back and make sure you do. Practice the vocabulary and idioms in your conversations, and look for them when reading different materials. Make sure to keep a balance when finding a partner by looking for the characteristics you want, while watching for red flags as you get to know the person. How is dating in the United States different than in your country? That would be an interesting conversation to have with a friend.

CHAPTER 18

Movies and Television

After reading this chapter, you should know more about . . .

- **Movie theaters**
- **Netflix**
- **On-demand**
- **Vocabulary related to watching movies and television, such as the following:**
    - Concession stand
    - Navigate
    - Reality TV

Movie Theaters

Americans are not going to the movies as often as they used to. For one, the ticket and concession stand prices have become very high. If you go to an IMAX theater, watch a 3-D or 4-D movie, or go to a theater with reclining seats, the ticket price is even higher. By the time you pay for your movie ticket, a drink, and some popcorn, you may have spent $25 or more. If you want candy, too, it could be $30 for just one person to have the full movie theater experience. Then there is the issue of the number of movie selections. If you try to watch a movie at home, you might have thousands of choices depending on whether you have cable, Netflix, or another service you subscribe to. Many people now also have large-screen televisions, which adds to their desire to stay home. Despite the drawbacks of going to the movies, it is a special experience. You can see a big movie premiere with fellow fans, hear the entire audience laugh or scream at the same time, enjoy a large screen that probably does not compare to the one you have at home, and engage in a discussion with friends after the movie is over. Those things might not be able to be replicated at home.

DIALOGUE 1

Let's see where Juan and Sofia decided to go to watch a movie.

Juan: Did you hear they are bringing *Justice League* to the theaters in 4-D?

Sofia: No, I didn't! I remember when we watched our first 3-D movie; it felt like we were in the room with the characters.

Juan: And with 4-D we'll feel like we are moving around with them, too. What do you think? Do you want to go see it in 4-D?

Sofia: Yeah, sure. I guess we should eat before we go. Right?

Juan: That's a good idea. That way we don't have to pay an arm and a leg while we're there.

Sofia: And the popcorn was soggy last time anyway.

Juan: Oh, yeah, I remember that.

Sofia: If we forget about going to the concession stand, we'll save a lot of money.

Juan: Money I don't have, so that's fine with me!

Sofia: The next show is at 4:30, so let's get something quick to eat and go.

concession stand: a place where you buy food and drinks—for example, at a movie theater. Example: We can go to the concession stand to get some popcorn.

IMAX theater: a theater that has a very large screen and seats that are at a sharp angle so you get a better view of the screen; a typical IMAX screen is 72.2 feet x 52.8 feet (22 meters x 16.1 meters); IMAX stands for *image maximum*. Example: I would like to see *Wonder Woman* in an IMAX theater so we can see it on the large screen.

3-D movie: a three-dimensional movie that enhances the illusion of depth perception and for which you wear special glasses. Example: I felt like I was being poked by the actors in that 3-D movie.

4-D movie: a 3-D movie that also has physical effects, such as the chairs moving or wind blowing on you. Example: The wind in that 4-D movie really made me feel like I was in the jungle with the actors.

selections: options available. Example: There are many movie selections at the local theater.

subscribe: pay to use services, such as to watch movies. Example: We should subscribe to Netflix so that we can watch more movies from home.

drawbacks: negative aspects or disadvantages of something. Example: One of the drawbacks of going to the movies is not being able to pause the movie so you can go to the bathroom.

movie premiere: the first day a movie is shown. Example: We should go to the movie premiere on Friday.

audience: people watching, or viewers. Example: In scary movies the audience can get very loud.

replicate: copy or reproduce. Example: You can't replicate the experience of watching a movie with a large audience at home.

pay an arm and a leg: an idiom that means to pay a lot of money for something. Example: He paid an arm and a leg for her birthday gift.

WRITE IT DOWN

What is your favorite movie? Where did you last see it? Tell us a story about this experience using two or more of the vocabulary words you just learned.

_____

_____

_____

_____

_____

_____

_____

_____

(Answers will vary.)

Fill in the blanks with the most appropriate vocabulary words or idioms you just learned.

1. With so many movie _____ , it can be hard to decide what to see.

2. I don't want to _____ an arm and a leg for one evening out.

3. He likes that the _____ stand has lots of candy.

4. I wanted to see that _____ movie because I heard that it made you feel like you were about to be eaten by the dinosaurs.

5. She plans to _____ to Netflix so that she can watch more movies from home.

6. I didn't realize how huge an _____ theater movie screen is.

7. You cannot easily _____ the experience of watching a movie with a big screen and large audience at home.

8. The _____ movie experience brings to life the movie beyond what you see.

9. There was a large _____ at the movie, so the screams got pretty loud.

10. I can't wait until Friday for the movie _____ .

(Answers are on page 251.)

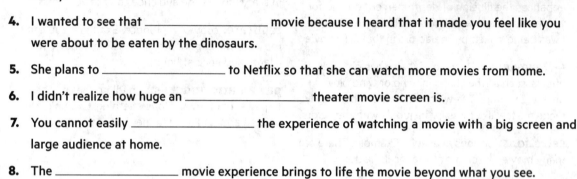

Netflix

Did you know you can watch Netflix in over 190 countries? For that reason, among others, it is one of the best streaming services. It has genres such as drama, comedy, sci-fi, action, horror, fantasy, and documentaries. You can also easily stream movies on your computer, iPad or other tablet, or phone at any time if you download the Netflix app. In addition, Netflix is creating many of its own television series, which cannot be viewed through any other website. Plus, all of its movies and shows are commercial-free. Some of the downsides are that you won't get to see the movies that just came out and that you need a high-speed Internet connection to view them. Netflix offers free trials, so you can decide for yourself if you like it. Hulu and Amazon offer similar services.

streaming service: an on-demand entertainment source that allows you to watch movies and/or television shows instantly for a fee (usually monthly) without having to download them. Example: It is nice to have streaming services when you have to go on a trip and are sitting around for a while.

genres: categories of movies, literature, or art. Example: There are many genres, but my favorite is comedy.

drama: a movie that is about a serious subject and is not intended to make the audience laugh. Example: I enjoy dramas because I am a serious person.

comedy: a movie that has humor and is intended to make the audience laugh. Example: A good comedy will have you laughing throughout the movie.

sci-fi: a movie that uses science fiction subjects, such as aliens and time travel. Example: It seems like there have been more sci-fi movies with time travel lately.

action: a movie in which the characters are nearly constantly in motion, such as in chases or fights that usually include violence. Example: After watching some action movies, you might feel exhausted from all of the chases.

horror: a scary movie. Example: It seems that many horror movies use music to create the scary mood.

fantasy: a movie that includes magic as part of its theme. Example: The *Harry Potter* movies would be considered fantasy because the film includes lots of magic throughout.

documentaries: nonfiction movies that teach you about something (for example, an event), someone, or a group of people. Example: The PBS channel is known for its informative documentaries.

downside: negative aspect or disadvantage of something. Example: A downside of watching movies at home is not having a huge screen.

MATCHING

Match the following words to their definitions using the vocabulary you just learned.

A. Drama
B. Streaming service
C. Sci-fi
D. Action
E. Comedy
F. Genres
G. Downside
H. Documentaries
I. Horror
J. Fantasy

1. _____ an on-demand entertainment source that allows you to watch movies and/or television shows instantly for a fee (usually monthly) without having to download them

2. _____ categories of movies, literature, or art

3. _____ a movie that is about a serious subject and is not intended to make the audience laugh

4. _____ a movie that has humor and is intended to make the audience laugh

5. _____ a movie that uses science fiction, such as aliens and time travel

6. _____ a movie in which the characters are nearly constantly in motion, such as in chases or fights that usually include violence

7. _____ a scary movie

8. _____ nonfiction movies that teach you about something (for example, an event), someone, or a group of people

9. _____ negative aspect or disadvantage

10. _____ a movie that includes magic as part of its theme

(Answers are on page 251.)

DIALOGUE 2

Let's see what genres Sofia and Juan prefer as they try to pick a movie to watch at Sofia's apartment. Can you guess?

Sofia: I like all types of movies.

Juan: Yes, but you know you have your favorites.

Sofia: I guess if I had to pick, I would say comedies are my favorite, followed by dramas.

Juan: I knew it!

Sofia: Let me guess your favorite. Sci-fi?

Juan: Yes. That's right. I can watch sci-fi movies all day and never get bored of them.

Sofia: Sci-fi movies often have a huge cast, like the next *Avengers* movie.

Juan: I think I'm ready for another movie. We saw my choice last time. What will your choice be?

Sofia: Let's look for a drama that will tug at your heartstrings.

Juan: Are you sure you don't want to look for a good comedy?

Sofia: Okay, that works for me, too. Let me scroll through Netflix to find a good one.

Juan: If you want me to navigate, just let me know.

Sofia: Nope, I have it under control. Thanks!

cast: the actors playing roles in a movie or television show. Example: The cast of any movie can be found on *imdb.com*.

tug at your heartstrings: an idiom that means something that makes you feel sympathy or love. Example: The scene where the guy rescues a child will tug at your heartstrings.

scroll: to move the text or images on a computer or television screen so that you can see different parts of the screen. Example: Please scroll through a little quicker so you can get to the comedy section.

navigate: to control the screen to get to the desired destination. Example: It is my turn to navigate, so please give me the remote control.

Which movie genre do you prefer and why? Tell us about the type of actors it has, and if you have a favorite actor, and then share this with a friend.

_____

_____

_____

_____

_____

(Answers will vary.)

Idioms About Television, Movies, and Shows

Have you heard the idioms below? Circle the ones that are new to you.

the show must go on	an event or activity that should continue even if there is a problem
channel surfing	looking through the television channels and then switching from show to show without watching an entire show
run the show	to be in charge
be on the edge of your seat	to be in suspense; closely following the action and excitement of something (for example, a performance)
behind the scenes	out of public view; without receiving credit or fame
steal the show	to get all the attention and praise
feel-good movie	a movie that makes you feel good
clean up your act	start doing good things instead of bad things
dog and pony show	a presentation created carefully to impress others
set the stage	prepare to do something
hard act to follow	a performance or presentation that is so outstanding that the next performance or presentation will not seem as good as if it were viewed on its own
act out	misbehave
break a leg	wish someone good luck
binge watch	watch a whole season of a show in one day
bring the house down	when the audience laughs and or claps intensely

Idiom Crossword

Complete the crossword below using the idioms you just learned.

ACROSS

2. There is a lot of work to be done behind the ____ that goes unnoticed.

5. Let me set the ____ for you so that you can better understand it.

6. That action movie keeps you on the ____ of your seat.

9. She might bring the house ____ with her super performance.

11. They had quite the ____ and pony show prepared for the big boss.

13. She is really a hard act to ____ because she is the best we have had.

15. If someone tells you to clean up your ____, you should probably do it.

DOWN

1. I can easily ____ watch that series because it is that good.

3. He kept ____ surfing, so we never did watch an entire show.

4. She wanted to ____ the show and be the star for once.

7. He wanted to watch a feel-____ movie because he was depressed.

8. He told me to break a ____ before I left to do the presentation.

10. He wanted to run the ____, so she let him take over.

12. She was having issues finishing her project, but the show must go ____.

14. His son started to act ____ in the middle of the movie.

(Answers are on page 251.)

STORY TIME

ON DEMAND

Juan wanted to watch his favorite television series on demand. He was looking forward to the possibility once he finished the spring semester at school. However, when he went to find his show, it was only available for a fee, and not all of the episodes were available. He was very upset. He had been dreaming of binge watching it. Fortunately, he had extra time to browse *through the selections and found a few new shows he had never seen that he quickly realized were just as interesting. His* demeanor *was once again positive as he sat and* devoured *episode after episode. The only problem he ran into was the need to buy some food. After watching television for hours, he realized he needed to eat. He quickly ran out to get some fast food so that he could come right back and continue with his shows. Before he knew it, time had flown by and the sun was rising. Luckily, it was the weekend and he didn't have to work.*

1. What happened to Juan at first?

    A. He missed his show.

    B. He couldn't watch his show.

    C. His show was not available.

2. What does it mean that he was able to browse?

    A. Jump through

    B. Look through

    C. Think through

3. What does demeanor mean?

    A. Behavior

    B. Happy

    C. Upset

4. What did he devour?

    A. Pizza

    B. Cheeseburgers

    C. Episodes

5. When he "ran out," he

    A. went running.

    B. went outside.

    C. went to get food.

(Answers are on page 252.)

browse: to look for or read something. Example: I want to browse the titles to find a good movie to watch.

demeanor: noticeable behavior. Example: His demeanor changed after watching the sad movie.

devoured: to eat quickly or enjoy with a passion (in the story he enjoyed the shows quickly). Example: She devoured the entire season in one weekend.

episode: one installment of a television show; usually there is one episode released each week during a show's season. Example: I think we have time to watch one episode because it is only 50 minutes long.

WRITE IT DOWN

What TV shows do you watch? Do you ever binge watch them? Tell us about your favorite episode and why it is your favorite. Include the setting, or where it takes place, in your description.

_____

_____

_____

_____

_____

(Answers will vary.)

Write TRUE or FALSE after the following sentences.

_____ **1.** Going to the movies can be expensive.

_____ **2.** An IMAX theater always has 4-D movies.

_____ **3.** Tickets for reclining seats cost more than regular seats.

_____ **4.** There are more selections on Netflix than at the movies.

_____ **5.** People are going to the movies more often now.

_____ **6.** Binge watching television often is not healthy.

_____ **7.** A movie's cast is important to the success of the movie.

_____ **8.** A 3-D movie requires glasses.

_____ **9.** A movie premiere is a highly rated movie.

_____ **10.** When you stream a movie, you download it.

(Answers are on page 252.)

Chapter Reflection

The following is a summary of what was covered in this chapter, including movie theaters, Netflix, and on demand. Hopefully you will browse through your (or your friend's) Netflix account and find a great show that will keep you coming back for more.

Vocabulary

concession stand	replicate	documentaries
IMAX theater	streaming service	downside
3-D movie	genres	cast
4-D movie	drama	scroll
selections	comedy	navigate
subscribe	sci-fi	browse
drawbacks	action	demeanor
movie premiere	horror	devoured
audience	fantasy	episode

Idioms

pay an arm and a leg

clean up your act

tug at your heartstrings

dog and pony show

the show must go on

set the stage

channel surfing

hard act to follow

run the show

act out

edge of your seat

break a leg

behind the scenes

binge watch

steal the show

bring the house down

feel-good movie

Do you remember all of the information covered in this chapter? If not, go back and review it to make sure you do. Practice the vocabulary and idioms in your conversations, and look for them when you are reading different materials. Look online to see if there are any 3-D or 4-D movies playing near you, and go see one if you can. Look around at the different theaters to go to the one with the best prices.

CHAPTER 19

Social Media

After reading this chapter, you should know more about . . .

- **How and why to use social media**

- **Facebook**

- **Instagram**

- **Twitter**

- **Pinterest**

- **Vocabulary related to social media, such as the following:**

    - Post

    - Profile picture

    - News feed

How and Why Do People Use Social Media?

Social media is very popular in the United States, as it is in many places around the world. Social media is a phrase used to describe the websites or mobile apps that allow people to share information with one another. Many people like to use social media to keep in touch with friends and family. They also use social media as a way to keep up with current events in popular—or pop—culture. Some people use social media to share and stay connected with people and events related to their job or field of work. See the following example of a conversation about using social media.

DIALOGUE 1

Juan: Are you on Facebook, Sofia? I want to join because my friends and family keep asking me if I've seen their pictures on Facebook and I'm tired of saying no.

Sofia: Of course I'm on Facebook. Isn't everyone?

Juan: Very funny. Well, maybe you can help me get started.

Sofia: Sure! First, let's go to Facebook on your computer and get you signed up. Just fill in all of the information for signing up.

Juan: Okay, I've got all the information in except the password. What should I pick?

Sofia: Facebook says you should use at least six **characters**, and that some of the characters should be numbers, letters, and punctuation marks.

Juan: Hmm . . . I think I've got one.

Sofia: You're doing great! Now, let me help you set up your **Facebook profile**.

Juan: Thanks! What's a Facebook profile?

Sofia: Your Facebook profile tells everyone about you.

Juan: Okay. I'll have to work on that a little. What do I need to do after that?

Sofia: Then you pick your **profile picture**. Your profile picture is the picture that people see when they connect to your Facebook.

Juan: Tell me more about sharing and **posting**.

Sofia: First, let me show you how to add friends on Facebook. It's really easy. Once you are on your **timeline**, all you have to do is enter a friend's name, email, or phone number in the search bar at the top. Click their name to go to their profile. Then, click "Add Friend." That sends them a **friend** request.

Juan: Okay, I just added you as my first friend on Facebook! Soon I can **follow** you and all our friends on Facebook. Thanks for your help!

Sofia: It was my pleasure!

post: to place a comment, message, or picture on a social media site. Example: James will post the pictures from his birthday tomorrow.

characters: letters, numbers, punctuation marks, and other symbols (for example, @, $, %, &). Example: You need to use at least six different characters for your password.

Facebook profile: a personal page on Facebook that tells others about you and your interests, hobbies, and any other information you want to share. Example: Lucia just started working on her Facebook profile.

profile picture: the picture everyone sees to identify you on Facebook. Example: You should pick a picture that you want everyone to see for your profile picture.

cover photo: the larger photo at the top of your Facebook profile, above your profile picture. Example: Sandra chose a picture of her family for the cover picture.

friend: on Facebook specifically, a friend is someone you share your profile with; to friend someone on Facebook means that you send the person a request to be your Facebook friend. Example: Did you friend the girl you met yesterday?

timeline: where you share your photos, posts, and experiences on Facebook. Example: If you look at his timeline, you can see he goes out a lot.

WRITE IT DOWN 1

Write a Facebook status message, using vocabulary from this or previous chapters. Try to work in an idiom, too!

_____

_____

_____

_____

_____

(Answers will vary.)

MATCHING

Match the following words to their definitions.

A. Timeline
B. Friend
C. Post
D. Cover photo
E. Profile picture
F. Characters
G. Facebook profile

1. _____ place a picture, comment, or message on a social media site

2. _____ a larger photo at the top of your profile, above your profile picture

3. _____ letters, numbers, punctuation marks, and symbols

4. _____ the place where you share your photos, posts, and experiences

5. _____ someone you share your profile with

6. _____ tells about you and your interests, hobbies, and other information you want to share

7. _____ the picture everyone sees to identify you on Facebook

(Answers are on page 252.)

Juan: Would you help me get started with making some posts?

Sofia: Sure! Like they say on Facebook, "What's on your mind?"

Juan: Ha! I noticed it says that by my profile picture. Is that how you post something?

Sofia: Yes! Why don't you start with posting a picture and saying something about it?

Juan: Okay, that sounds good.

Sofia: Let's open your news feed.

Juan: Wow! There's a lot there. I'm going to have to limit how much time I spend with this.

Sofia: Social media can take up a lot of your time, if you let it. Now, click on "What's on your mind?" and click on the camera icon to add the picture from your phone.

Juan: That was easy!

Sofia: And, if you see something you like, you can just tap the like button. You'll see they also have other different reactions you can choose from: love, haha, wow, sad, and angry.

Juan: That seems fun!

Sofia: One piece of advice I would give you is never to post anything on Facebook that you wouldn't want a future boss or your parents to see. That goes for commenting on other people's posts, too. I try to stick to positive, upbeat topics when I post something, and I just don't comment if I can't say something positive to someone else. You don't want to be a troll. You can also check your privacy settings to set who sees your posts.

Juan: Noted! Actually, another friend told me this, too.

news feed: a frequently updated list of stories, apps, pictures, pages, groups, and video links seen on your Facebook homepage. Example: If you have not been on Facebook for a while, you can look at the news feed for hours because there will be so many posts.

like: showing positive feedback for things you have seen others post. Example: My friend always asks me to like all of her posts.

comment: saying something about what you saw on a post or in the news feed on Facebook. Example: I like it when people comment on my pictures.

troll: a person who makes comments online to anger people for fun. Example: I don't like him because he is a troll.

What's on your mind?: a section on your Facebook page next to your cover photo where you can make a comment, include a photo or video, tag friends, check in, or place an icon describing your feelings and activities. Example: She needs to go to the "What's on your mind?" section of Facebook to post that.

social media: a phrase to describe the websites and applications, or apps, used to allow people to share information (including photos and videos) with one another. Example: Facebook is a very popular social media website for talking to people.

icon: a small picture that stands for something (for example, a speech bubble for commenting on a post). Example: She could not find the camera icon to post her vacation pictures.

reaction: the different icons (also called emojis) used to express how you feel about a post on Facebook. Example: He used the sad reaction to show how he felt about them moving away.

What two pieces of advice did
Sofia give to Juan about safety
and the time spent on Facebook?
Why do you think they are
important to keep in mind?

_____

_____

_____

_____

_____

_____

_____

(Answers will vary. Sample answer is on page 252.)

Next, use the following words in a sentence.

icon: _____

_____

reaction: _____

_____

comment: _____

_____

news feed: _____

_____

like: _____

_____

(Answers will vary.)

_____ **1.** A profile picture is the same as a cover photo.

_____ **2.** A post is when you place a statement or comment on your Facebook page.

_____ **3.** A news feed is a newspaper article.

_____ **4.** Social media includes television.

_____ **5.** A drawing of a camera can be an icon.

_____ **6.** You give a reaction after you read a post, news feed, or comment.

(Answers are on page 252.)

Idioms Related to Social Media

As you have learned, idioms are phrases that do not make sense when you translate them literally but are used all of the time. Therefore, it is a good idea to learn them in order to understand languages more easily. Below is a list of many idioms related to social media.

grow your following	an expression that means you take steps or actions to increase the number of people who view your posts and comments
surfing the net	when Internet users go to a variety of sites, blogs, or news feeds
going viral	the rapid spread of information, ideas, or trends by means of social media; for example, a video of a dancing baby has gone viral once it's been viewed by millions of people
lost in cyberspace	when something is on the Internet but cannot be found (*cyberspace* refers to the Internet)
down to a science	doing something in the best, fastest, or most logical way
ahead of the curve	when someone says or does something that is advanced compared to most others

Complete each sentence by using one of the idioms related to social media that you just learned.

1. I couldn't find that article on the Internet. It must be lost in _____ .

2. If you can get more people to your Facebook page, you can probably grow your _____ .

3. A lot of people spend large amounts of time just surfing the _____ .

4. A lot of people have thought of ways to search for something on the Internet, but I think my friend's method is ahead of the _____ .

5. That video I took of my dog is so cute that if I sent it to enough people, it would probably start going _____ .

6. She is so quick at posting things on Facebook; she must have it down to a _____ .

(Answers are on page 252.)

DIALOGUE 3

Juan: I've been having fun on Facebook, and so far I've been keeping it to 10 to 15 minutes a day. Now friends are asking me if I'm on Instagram and Twitter. What can you tell me about those?

Sofia: They are other forms of social media.

Juan: So, what is Instagram? I've noticed that sometimes when my friends post pictures on Facebook, it says it's an Instagram picture.

Sofia: Instagram is a fun way to share with friends through a series of pictures. Take a photo with your phone, and then you can choose a filter to change the look of the picture and make it stand out. You can add a caption, too. Instagram photos can be shared on Facebook and even Twitter at the same time if you want.

Juan: That sounds like fun! What about Twitter? How is that different from Instagram and Facebook? I'm so behind on this social media stuff!

Sofia: Twitter is a social networking service where users post short 140-character messages called tweets. It can be a little confusing at first, but Twitter has a great "help section" for new users. For example, it tells you how to use a hashtag.

Juan: You use Twitter, don't you?

Sofia: Yeah, I like to follow certain people and topics. On Twitter and Instagram, instead of friends, you have followers.

Juan: Okay, maybe if you help me sign up for Instagram and Twitter, I'll start by following you and my other friends to see how it works.

Sofia: Sure! That sounds like a good plan.

hashtag: a word or phrase after the # symbol that categorizes the accompanying text. Example: When you click on a hashtag, you will see other tweets that have the same keyword or topic.

tweet: a short message on the social networking site Twitter that has up to 140 characters. Example: Even though a tweet is not very long, it can be very powerful.

followers: other Twitter users who have subscribed to your tweets or messages so they can receive and read them. Example: She does not have very many Twitter followers.

Which type of social media would you most likely use to do the following (Facebook, Instagram, and/or Twitter)?

1. I would like to send a short message to one of my friends.

   _____

2. I would like to send a funny picture to my sister.

   _____

3. I want to see what topics my friends are posting about.

   _____

4. I have an opinion I would like to share with all my friends.

   _____

5. I changed the appearance of my dog and want to send a photo to my friends.

   _____

6. I want to read all the short messages my favorite music group sent after the concert.

   _____

(Answers are on page 252.)

STORY TIME

REDECORATING

Sofia went over to Juan's house late in the afternoon. Juan's mother said she could tell he was in his room by all the noise she could hear downstairs. "It sounds like an earthquake up there! He is usually sitting quietly at his desk working on the computer. Why don't you go up and see what's going on?"

Sofia knocked on the door, and the noise stopped. When Juan let her in, she said, "Hi, what's up?" Juan said that now that he was spending more time in his room working on all the new social media he was using, his room was getting too messy, even for him.

Sofia smiled and said, "Yes, I see what you mean." It was Juan's turn to smile now.

"I'm tired of not being able to find anything. I have no place to put all my stuff, and my desk is a mess!" Sofia then suggested that he might want to try one more Internet site to help him. Juan cried, "You mean I need to know about another social media site?"

Sofia said, "Well, not exactly. Have you heard of Pinterest?"

Juan said, "I've heard of it, but I don't know what it is."

Sofia replied, "It's a great site to find out information and ideas about a lot of things. You can use it without really participating in sharing information yourself. Let's go to www.pinterest.com on your computer and search for "organizing bedrooms." When Juan and Sofia got on the site, they could scroll down and see hundreds of pictures and ideas for bedrooms. Juan was excited about all of the choices.

Sofia said, "Look at the one that says, 'Guide on How to Organize Rooms for Guys.'"

Juan said, "That's perfect! I'm going to save that page and spend some time looking at all the different ideas. How about if I make some choices and share them with you tomorrow?"

Sofia said, "Sounds like a plan, see you tomorrow!"

1. Why was Juan's mom surprised by the noise coming from Juan's room?

_____

_____

_____

2. What was Juan's problem in the story?

_____

_____

_____

3. What was Juan's first reaction to hearing about Pinterest?

_____

_____

_____

4. How is Pinterest different from the other sites that Sofia and Juan visited?

_____

_____

_____

(Answers are on page 252.)

Vocabulary Crossword

Complete the crossword below using the vocabulary you just learned.

ACROSS

2. A word or phrase after the # symbol

3. Other Twitter users who have followed you to read your tweets

7. Where you share your photos, posts, and experiences on Facebook

8. A site with information and pictures

9. A person's personal page on Facebook

DOWN

1. Symbols such as letters, numbers, and punctuation marks

4. A short message having up to 140 characters

5. An emoji on Facebook to show your emotional response to a post

6. To place a comment, message, or picture on a social media site

10. A symbol, drawing, or object used on a page, news feed, or comment

(Answers are on page 252.)

Chapter Reflection

The following is a summary of what was covered in this chapter, from how and why to use social media to the details of Facebook, Instagram, Twitter, and Pinterest. If you have not tried all of these yet, pick one to try today!

Vocabulary

post	like	social media
friend	comment	icon
Facebook profile	hashtag	reaction
profile picture	tweet	troll
cover photo	followers	
news feed	characters	
timeline	What's on your mind?	

Idioms

grow your following

surfing the net

going viral

lost in cyberspace

down to a science

ahead of the curve

Do you remember all of the information covered in this chapter? If not, go back and review it to make sure you do. Practice the vocabulary and idioms in your conversations, and look for them when reading different materials. If you are already on these social media sites, do some research about how to get more followers, and see how you do. Be sure to make an effort to meet with your friends and family in person, too.

CHAPTER 20

Computer and Mobile Applications: YouTube, Websites, and Apps

After reading this chapter, you should know more about . . .

- **Learning how to navigate and use YouTube**

- **Building vocabulary and idioms online or through apps**

- **Vocabulary related to computer technology, such as the following:**

    - Upload

    - Launch

    - Copyright

YouTube

YouTube is a video-sharing website created in 2005 by three men who all had previously worked at **PayPal**. They wanted to let people easily **upload** videos to watch and share. One year later, in 2006, when the website had become very popular, it was sold to Google for $1.6 billion!

Visitors to the website can see video clips, **classic** and current TV shows, music videos, and movie **trailers**. The site also has short films, **documentaries**, and educational videos. The educational videos show how to do a range of things, from cooking to repairing various **consumer** products.

Since its 2005 **launch**, YouTube has added several additional websites. YouTube Kids was launched in 2015. Parents can control the available content. They also have a YouTube Gaming site. Most of their videos are free, but they also offer a site called YouTube Red. It requires a fee and **subscription** for **premium** channels, no ads, and additional content.

DIALOGUE 1

Let's see what Bob and Tracey look for on YouTube in the following dialogue.

Bob: Yesterday, **out of the blue**, I had a sudden desire to watch one of my favorite childhood shows. I couldn't find it on Netflix though.

Tracey: You should try YouTube! I've found some of the classics that I watched when I was younger. It really brings back memories, although I wouldn't **rate** all of them highly.

Bob: YouTube! I hadn't thought of that. I have mostly been listening to music on it.

Tracey: Well, I usually use Spotify to listen to music. I don't pay for it, so I have to listen to some commercials.

Bob: You know, we could pay for YouTube Red so that we can watch YouTube's original shows and other videos without ads.

Tracey: That sounds great! I've heard some are really good.

PayPal: a secure website for sending and receiving payments through the Internet. Example: When I ordered my sister's birthday present, I used PayPal instead of a credit card.

upload: to send information (for example, text or pictures) from a computer or phone to a website or other computer. Example: I want to upload my vacation pictures to my Facebook news feed.

classic: refers to content that was created in the past and is recognized for its popularity or quality. Example: That movie we saw last night was so good; I think it will become a classic.

trailers: short previews of movies that usually include a series of scenes from the movie. Example: The trailer for the new superhero movie looked exciting.

documentaries: films or shows that provide information about a particular topic and can include photos, video clips, and interviews. Example: The documentary I saw about Abraham Lincoln was riveting.

consumer: a person who purchases goods, information, or services. Example: As a consumer, I always want to read reviews on things before I buy them.

launch: put a new website on the Internet, put a new product on the market, or send something up in the air (for example, launch a rocket). Example: The company said it would launch its new website at the beginning of next month.

subscription: a paid service that allows you to receive either printed or electronic material on a regular basis, such as a newspaper or magazine. Example: My subscription to my favorite magazine is about to end.

premium: an amount paid above what is usual, often in order to get some added benefit. Example: You can pay a premium to get front-row seats.

out of the blue: an idiom that means something unexpected or surprising. Example: She decided out of the blue to finish all of her homework for the week.

rate: to judge content, such as a movie, song, or website. Example: I would rate last night's play as great—five stars!

WRITE IT DOWN

Describe a least three things you can see or do on YouTube. If you are not sure, look around on YouTube and come back to tell us.

_____

_____

_____

_____

_____

_____

(Answers will vary.)

Fill in the blanks with the most appropriate vocabulary words you just learned.

1. I learned a lot from watching the _____ on TV about the history of computers.
2. My sister received an email telling her that her _____ to her favorite magazine was ending soon.
3. Our school is ready to _____ a brand-new version of its website.
4. Our teacher told us the book we were going to read in class was written fifty years ago and was considered to be a _____ .
5. Later, I plan to _____ the pictures from our camping trip onto Facebook.
6. My friend said that, to be safe, I should use _____ to buy my new shoes on the Internet.
7. After watching several _____ , we decided which movie we wanted to see.
8. As a _____ , you have to carefully decide how to spend your money.
9. In order for customers to avoid having to view commercials, they are charged a _____ by the website.
10. After buying something online, the company asked me to _____ my experience with the ordering process.

(Answers are on page 252.)

DIALOGUE 2

Tracey and Bob share some new things they discovered on YouTube.

Bob: Have you discovered anything new on YouTube? I've been having a great time watching those old shows.

Tracey: Actually, I have, because I have been procrastinating on finishing my project for our American Government class. So, I have been playing around with it a lot. But, remember how we didn't feel confident in that class earlier this year?

Bob: I sure do.

Tracey: Well, I'm starting to feel better about this project. First, I had to decide on a topic. I picked the struggle women had in getting the right to vote in the United States. I started to research that topic on Wikipedia, then decided to use some more reliable sources in the school library. When I thought I had enough information, I started to create my PowerPoint to show in class. Then I thought, "How could I make it really interesting to everyone in class?"

Bob: So, what did you do?

Tracey: I searched YouTube for videos on speeches and demonstrations that were given by people who were for women's voting rights and those who were against it. I also found some fascinating documentaries on the leaders of the suffrage movement.

Bob: Interesting. I know very little about that part of history.

Tracey: Did you know women didn't get the right to vote in the United States until 1920? Anyway, now I have to select what material I want to use and then see how I can use the YouTube videos in my PowerPoint.

Bob: I'll help you figure that out!

Tracey: That would be great!

procrastinating: finding excuses not to do something that needs to be said or done. Example: My father keeps procrastinating getting the lawn mower repaired.

confident: a feeling or an attitude that you have the ability to do something. Example: I am confident I could learn to play the piano if I studied and practiced enough.

Wikipedia: a free online encyclopedia that viewers can read and edit, which is okay for quick information but is not a reliable source since anyone can edit it. Example: I found an interesting history of photography on Wikipedia.

PowerPoint: a program designed to create presentations that show one or more pages of information called slides, which can contain words, pictures, and/or video clips. Example: I saw a great PowerPoint that explains how to apply for college.

fascinating: interesting, amazing, or unusual. Example: I read a fascinating description of how monkeys were taught sign language.

suffrage movement: a movement by women starting in the 1840s to give women the right to vote. Example: Susan B. Anthony was one of the leaders of the suffrage movement.

MATCHING

Match the following words to their definitions using the vocabulary you just learned.

A. Wikipedia
B. Suffrage movement
C. Confident
D. Procrastination
E. PowerPoint
F. Fascinating

1. _____ the movement that helped women get the right to vote

2. _____ a presentation program

3. _____ when you feel you have the ability to do something

4. _____ an online encyclopedia

5. _____ when something is very interesting

6. _____ when someone keeps putting off doing something

(Answers are on page 252.)

DOWNLOADING CONTENT FROM YOUTUBE

Tracey wants to add videos to her school PowerPoint project on women's suffrage. She thinks the videos would make the topic interesting to both the females and the males in her class. Bob has agreed to help her figure out how to do it. He searched the Internet for suggestions on how to download videos on YouTube. He found a great deal of information but didn't know what advice or suggestions to follow. What he learned was that it was not an easy, one-step procedure. Most sources advised downloading special applications to get the videos. Some of the videos would need to be converted in order to use them. He tried some applications, but some didn't work with his computer. Others were trial subscriptions that only lasted a short time. He also read about the need to follow copyright guidelines when copying material. He then decided there had to be an easier way to help Tracey.

After looking at some sites on how to do PowerPoints, he found just the information he needed at https://support.office.com. *It had a great video that explained the difference between downloading a video to embed in a PowerPoint and putting a link in a PowerPoint to a website that had the video. He decided that it would be easier for Tracey to put a link in her PowerPoint to the videos she found on YouTube.*

Let's see how much you remember from the story about downloading content from YouTube by answering the following true or false statements.

_____ **1.** Downloading content from YouTube or other sites is always very easy.

_____ **2.** To post a link or to embed a video mean the same thing.

_____ **3.** You need to have an Internet connection to follow links.

_____ **4.** A trial subscription is usually temporary.

_____ **5.** You need a web address to create a link.

_____ **6.** People should follow copyright guidelines.

(Answers are on page 252.)

sources: places where information can be found, such as websites, blogs, or books. Example: I had to look for many sources before I found the one I needed.

application: a computer program that performs specific tasks or activities, such as shopping, playing media, or editing photos. Example: To fix the photos, I needed to download a better photo-editing application.

convert: to change a file or document from one format or type to another. Example: When she tried to upload a picture, a popup message told her she needed to convert the photo to a jpeg file.

trial: used as a test for a period of time to see if something is worth buying or using. Example: He wanted to buy the program but decided to start with the trial version before committing.

copyright: a law that protects authors from having others copy or use their work, such as books, music, applications, and other types of original work. Example: Before he could use that picture on his website, he had to get copyright permission from the publisher.

embed: to place a picture, video, or web link in a document or PowerPoint. Example: You can add interest to a presentation if you embed pictures, cartoons, or videos.

link: a web address that has been inserted or embedded in an email, document, or presentation so you can click on the link and go to the website. Example: The website I visited had links to helpful information on how to repair my computer.

Useful Websites

There are many websites available to help people learn language, but some that you might find helpful are the Voice of America (VOA) Learning English (*http://learningenglish.voanews.com*) and the British Broadcasting Corporation (BBC) Learning English (*http://www.bbc.co.uk/learningenglish/english/*) sites. Both of these websites have different levels of English, so you can work at your level. The VOA and BBC have lessons with videos, podcasts, readings, activities, and quizzes on different topics. Simple English Wikipedia (*https://simple.wikipedia.org/wiki/Main_Page*) can be useful, too! It is like Wikipedia but made a little simpler for English learners. If you type "idioms" into the search box, you can have fun reading all sorts of funny-sounding sayings. And, if you really like idioms, look at the Idiom Site (*http://idiomsite.com/*) for even more. You just have to make sure to cross-check the information on other reliable websites because, just like Wikipedia, anyone can edit the information.

podcast: an audio file (like a music or news program) that you can download from the Internet onto your computer or phone. Example: She downloaded the podcast on VOA about finding free eBooks.

WRITE IT DOWN

Look into the websites just mentioned and share some of the things you liked about them and what you learned (or want to learn). What would you want to see that they did not provide? Write that down too.

_____

_____

_____

_____

_____

(Answers will vary.)

DIALOGUE 3

Read the following dialogue to see what Tracey and Bob learned on the VOA website, and notice how many idioms they use. Circle the idioms you know.

Tracey: Hey, Bob, did you know that Amazon has a lot of free eBooks?

Bob: Yeah, I read that. I also learned that you shouldn't download eBooks from just any website because you might also download a virus.

Tracey: Yeah, I read about that, too.

Bob: Another cool thing I found out was that some libraries have free eBooks you can get on the OverDrive website or app.

Tracey: To make a long story short, did you also hear you can get free books on the Google Play Store's free bestsellers, on the iBooks app, and through the Project Gutenberg website?

Bob: Ha, ha, ha! I guess we read the same article. Well, I won't be buying any books anytime soon with all of these free books available. I am really excited about this.

Tracey: You know, practice makes perfect, so if we listen and read a lot, we'll get great vocabularies.

Bob: That's true; we can learn on our own. This isn't rocket science.

Tracey: Agreed. No need to hit the panic button.

Bob: We could also play some games on apps to work on our vocabulary, like Words with Friends or Word Streak.

Tracey: I love playing Word Streak, and I've noticed that since my vocabulary has gotten better, I am getting higher scores.

Bob: Cool! I'll have to invite you to play a game so I can beat you!

Idioms from This Chapter

The following idioms are related to this chapter. Circle the idioms that you already know from the list.

bells and whistles	when something comes with all of the extras
out of the blue	something unexpected or surprising
to make a long story short	to be brief or to get to the point
hitting the panic button	becoming really worried
practice makes perfect	getting better at doing something through repetition
reinvent the wheel	to create something that has already been created

STOP AND THINK 2

Complete each sentence by using one of the idioms from this chapter.

1. I couldn't think of the address, and then suddenly I could. It just came to me out of the _____ .

2. Since he didn't have much time left to make his comments, he was told to make a _____ story short.

3. I know you are worried about finishing your class project, but don't start hitting the panic _____ .

4. The more you use the Internet, the easier it is to find what you need because _____ makes perfect.

5. That computer has all of the bells and _____ , which is why it costs so much.

6. You don't need to reinvent the _____ because there is already an app for that.

(Answers are on page 252.)

Vocabulary Crossword

Complete the crossword below using the vocabulary you just learned.

ACROSS

2. A law protecting an individual's work
4. A web address placed in a document that will take you to the site being linked
5. Being sure of yourself
7. A presentation program for creating presentations
9. Very interesting or amazing
10. A computer program that performs a specific task

DOWN

1. An online encyclopedia that users can read and edit
3. Finding excuses not to do something
6. Placing a file or document into another file or document
8. To change something from one format or type to another

(Answers are on page 252.)

Chapter Reflection

The following is a summary of what was covered in this chapter, which included information about YouTube, websites, and apps to help build your vocabulary and idioms related to computer and mobile technologies. You should find a free eBook on one of the suggested websites and start reading or listening to it today!

Vocabulary

PayPal	premium	sources
upload	rate	application
classic	procrastinating	convert
trailers	confident	trial
documentaries	Wikipedia	copyright
consumer	PowerPoint	embed
launch	fascinating	link
subscription	suffrage movement	

Idioms

bells and whistles	to make a long story short
reinvent the wheel	hitting the panic button
out of the blue	practice makes perfect

Do you remember all of the information covered in this chapter? If not, go back and review it to make sure you do. Practice the vocabulary words in your conversations, and look for them when reading different materials. Think about something you want to learn how to do, such as how to fix something in your house, and look it up on YouTube to see how much you can do on your own. For example, if there is something you have been meaning to fix, find out how on YouTube and then try it yourself.

CHAPTER 21

Keeping Up with the News

After reading this chapter, you should know more about . . .

- **A variety of both digital and traditional (paper) news sources**

- **News on television, including TV websites**

- **How to decide whether a news article is true**

- **Vocabulary related to the news, such as the following:**

    - Bias

    - Point of view

    - Editorial

Today's News

If you want to keep up with what is going on in the world, there are many ways to do so, whether you are interested in news from your neighborhood, town, state, or country, or are more intrigued by global issues. There are both traditional and digital sources of news available today. Traditional sources include newspapers, magazines, and newsletters. Newspapers and magazines can provide information about local, state, national, and world news. Newsletters usually talk about what is happening locally, such as in a community, church, or club. There are also many digital sources of news. These would include websites, news feeds, blogs, and social media. Many of the traditional news sources also have websites that contain much of the same information that is available in their paper versions.

DIALOGUE 1

Let's see what Tracey and Bob are doing to get more involved with the news.

Tracey: What do you think of the American Government class we just took?

Bob: I thought some of our classmates seemed to be very knowledgeable about what was going on in the world. And sometimes I didn't even know what they were talking about. I was lost in that discussion about bias, point of view, and editorials.

Tracey: I didn't quite understand it either. Well, I have an idea to get up to speed with the news!

Bob: Okay, let's hear it!

Tracey: Why don't we start finding some news sites that will tell us what has been going on in the world?

Bob: That sounds like a great idea. How do you think we should start?

Tracey: Why don't we each find three or four sites that cover local, national, and world news? We can then compare our notes and decide which ones we like the best.

Bob: That sounds like a great plan. This will really help our grades.

traditional: practices, habits, and customs that have been used for a long time. Example: In the Newseum, a museum about print and electronic communication, there is a collection of traditional newspapers' front pages.

digital: computer or electronic technology. Example: He likes to read the news in a digital format on his phone.

blog: a website or web page with a diary-like feel that is updated regularly, usually by an individual or small group. Example: She worked on her cooking blog every day, adding one recipe a day.

knowledgeable: having a lot of information about a subject. Example: She is very knowledgeable about the space program.

bias: a tendency to think that some ideas or information are better, truer, or more accurate than others. Example: We all are biased about some things, so we need to continue to read and become more informed.

point of view: thinking about something in a certain way because of your background or experiences. Example: Her point of view will probably change as she gets older.

editorial: an article in a magazine or newspaper in which someone (usually an editor or publisher) expresses an opinion. Example: I always like to read the editorials to see if my opinion is similar to the editor's opinion.

get up to speed: an idiom that means having the latest information about a subject or event/activity. Example: She needs to get up to speed on the new computer program at work.

cover: to report news about specific people or places. Example: He will cover the latest from City Hall at 6 p.m. on the local news station.

WRITE IT DOWN

Explain the difference between traditional and digital sources of news. Then, explain which type of sources you prefer and why.

_____

_____

_____

_____

_____

_____

_____

_____

_____

(Answers will vary. Sample answer is on page 252.)

Use the new vocabulary to complete the following sentences.

1. Most of my friends don't use _____ sources of information because they think newspapers and magazines are old-fashioned.

2. I thought the opinions she expressed in her newspaper's _____ were similar to mine.

3. The reporter thought that the way he would _____ the traffic accident was to talk to the police and the people involved in the crash.

4. Her _____ about global warming was pretty obvious when she spoke to the class.

5. After reading nearly a dozen articles on how to keep in shape, I now feel fairly _____ .

6. My father took some of his old photographs to be converted to a _____ format so he could put them on his computer.

7. I accept that the coach's _____ of view about coming to practice might be different from that of the members of the team.

8. I really need to get up to _____ in using social media because all of my friends are.

(Answers are on page 252.)

News Sources

There are a number of news sources that are available in both traditional and digital **formats**. The oldest sources are newspapers and magazines. However, they are now also available in digital formats. Newspapers are exactly what their name means: news printed on paper. Newspapers report on not only the news but also on food, travel, sports, and entertainment, and they also contain advertisements. Newspapers are usually printed each day or once a week. Many people get their news from newspapers, such as:

The New York Times   *The Boston Herald*

The Washington Post   *The Miami Herald*

The Chicago Tribune   *The Seattle Times*

The LA Times   *USA Today*

The Wall Street Journal

Magazines can be printed weekly, monthly, or a few times a year. Most of the popular news magazines are also available in digital format. Here are some examples:

Newsweek   *Time*

Rolling Stone   *US News & World Report*

There are also news sources that are only online, such as Google News. On their website, you can read about top stories, world news, U.S. news, business, technology, entertainment, sports, science, and health. Within those topics, you can see numerous articles from different news sources. Plus, it keeps track of what you view and creates a section called "Suggested for You" based on what you have been clicking on. CNN and the Huffington Post are other popular places to look up news online. Some of the most popular news sources also have an additional site that is specifically for teens, such as CNN Student News, Huffington Post Teen, and Sports Illustrated for Kids.

> **format:** the way in which something is presented, such as online or on paper. Example: She likes to read the news in a digital format online.
>
> **top stories:** the most timely and important stories for the audience of a news outlet. Example: Some of today's top stories can be found in *USA Today.*

DIALOGUE 2

Tracey: I had a lot of fun searching for news sites online. How did you do?

Bob: I enjoyed the search, too, but I'm not sure I found the best sites. Let's compare what we found.

Tracey: I went to the library and found actual newspapers and a huge magazine section. I copied their names and then went on the computer and tried to see which ones had digital versions. All the ones I looked at had both paper and digital versions.

Bob: Which ones looked the best to you?

Tracey: I liked the *New York Times* and *USA Today* sites the best. They were easy to navigate and had a lot of articles that were interesting.

Bob: One thing I realized is that if you want to hear or see some breaking news, you have to turn on a TV or a radio, or go online. I liked listening to podcasts too. Did you find any good magazines?

Tracey: I thought *US News & World Report* would be a big help. I also liked *Kind News* because, as you know, I love all kinds of animals. What did you find?

Bob: I found some of the same ones. But I also found a couple of different ones I liked.

Tracey: Which were your favorites?

Bob: For newspapers, I agree with you that *USA Today* had great short articles on a lot of different topics. With magazines, I thought the pictures and articles in *Time* magazine were great. Since I like sports a lot, I also thought *Sports Illustrated* was great.

Tracey: Did you find any that can help us be more informed about the latest news?

Bob: The CNN News website *is* very helpful. I also thought the Huffington Post site was interesting. They had a really funny section called "Weird News."

breaking news: news about an event that has just happened. Example: Did you hear the breaking news about the storm that is coming our way?

podcasts: digital audio files that are available on the Internet and can be downloaded to a computer or mobile device and are often part of a series. Example: She likes to listen to the *This American Life* podcast on the way to work.

Believing What You Read

There is so much information available nowadays. Traditional sources like newspapers and magazines have been joined by an exploding number of news and opinion websites, blogs, and podcasts. Social media users are also giving their viewpoints on current events. How do you decide whether what you are reading is truthful and accurate? The following are some things you can do to be more confident in the accuracy of the news you are reading:

1. Look at the source of the news. Is it from someone who has an obvious bias or point of view? Is it from a source that includes different points of view on an issue?
2. Does the news provide sources for the facts it uses? Is there only one source, or are there multiple sources? Are the sources the opinions of other people, or are they based on a study or research?
3. Use fact-checker sites to get more information about an issue or statement. Some fact-checker sites include:

   www.factcheck.org
   www.opensecrets.org
   www.politifact.com
   www.snopes.com
   www.truthorfiction.com

4. If there is a controversial issue, try to look at both sides of the issue.

controversial: likely to give rise to a disagreement or dispute. Example: Whether or not Pete Rose should get into the National Baseball Hall of Fame is controversial because he gambled on baseball.

WRITE IT DOWN

What advice would you give to someone who wants to be better informed about the news? Where would you recommend they look and why?

_____

_____

_____

_____

_____

_____

_____

(Answers will vary.)

MATCHING

Match the following words to their definitions using the vocabulary and idioms you have learned.

A. Controversial

B. Breaking news

C. Blog

D. Format

E. Podcast

1. _____ a website with a diary-like feel run by a person or small group

2. _____ how something is presented, such as online or on paper

3. _____ news about an event that has just happened

4. _____ likely to give rise to a disagreement or argument

5. _____ a digital audio file available on the Internet that can be downloaded to a computer or smartphone

(Answers are on page 252.)

Vocabulary Crossword

Complete the crossword below using the vocabulary you just learned.

ACROSS

4. Computer or electronic technology
5. A website with a diary-like design, created by an individual or small group
6. To report news about specific people, or places, or topics
7. Having a lot of information about a topic
9. How something, such as the news, is presented (for example, online or on paper)

DOWN

1. A digital audio file on the Internet, usually part of a series
2. A paper magazine is a _____ source.
3. Likely to give rise to a disagreement or dispute
8. A statement in a magazine, newspaper, or online wherein which someone expresses an opinion

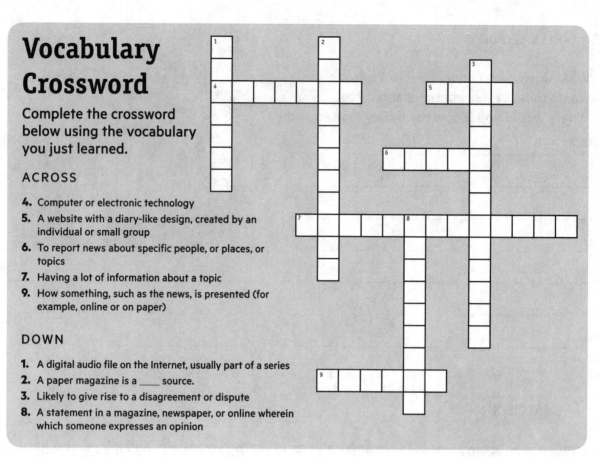

(Answers are on page 252.)

Idioms Related to News

The following are some idioms that may or may not be about the news but sound like they might be. Circle the idioms that are new to you.

word of mouth	when news or information is shared by people simply talking to other people
break the news	when someone shares the news, which is probably bad news
hot off the press	new information that has just been made public
no news is good news	when you don't hear from someone, you don't need to worry that something bad has happened
that's news to me	when you learn something new that is unexpected
bearer of bad news	a person who shares bad news
get the lowdown	learn the information
bad news travels fast	people talk about bad news often, so before you know it, many people will know about it
keep me posted	keep someone up to date with the latest information or news about something
heard it through the grapevine	learned about news or something through someone else

READING IN LINE

While waiting in line at the grocery store, Bob decided to read some of the magazines next to him. He thought it was funny how some magazines said really silly things. One said an alien took a family in the middle of the night, and another said a woman was having 15 babies at once. He couldn't believe it but wanted to find out if those stories were true, so he checked on snopes.com, where he found out those were false. He wondered how many people would get the lowdown on those magazines and believe it. He also thought about all of the controversial articles he saw and thought that it would be sad if people didn't check both sides of the story through other sources or even word of mouth. It was now time for him to purchase his items, so he added a newspaper that was hot off the press to his stack of items. He was looking forward to reading about other stories and finding out if they were true.

1. Was a woman having 15 babies at once?

    A. Yes

    B. No

2. What other websites could Bob have used to check the facts?

    A. *www.factcheck.org*

    B. *www.opensecrets.org*

    C. *www.politifact.com*

    D. All of the above

3. Bob looked at magazines and bought a newspaper. Where else might he find the news?

    A. Websites

    B. Blogs

    C. Podcasts

    D. All of the above

4. What does "hot off the press" mean?

    A. New information that has just been made public

    B. Something that is very hot

    C. Where things get printed

5. Why was Bob looking forward to reading about other stories?

    A. To find out more information

    B. To find out if the stories were real

    C. To learn about the mother with 15 babies

(Answers are on page 252.)

Fill in the blanks with the correct idiom.

1. He heard about the new school through _____ of mouth.

2. George said, "That's news to _____" when he heard that his friend was quitting his job.

3. She told him that if he didn't hear from her within a week, no news was _____ news.

4. She was able to _____ the news that she needed to move again without her family getting upset.

5. He was the _____ of bad news and told us they did not have any more chocolate cake for us.

6. The news about the 22-car crash is hot off the _____ .

7. She found out about the budget cuts the next day because _____ news travels fast.

8. Please keep me _____ about your next vacation.

9. She would like to get the _____ on what he is planning to do next.

10. When the party was cancelled, she heard it through the _____ .

(Answers are on page 252.)

Use the following idioms in a sentence that you might use while talking to a friend.

word of mouth

_____

break the news

_____

hot off the press

_____

no news is good news

_____

that's news to me

_____

bearer of bad news

_____

get the lowdown

_____

bad news travels fast

_____

keep me posted

_____

heard it through the grapevine

_____

(Answers will vary.)

Chapter Reflection

The following is a summary of what was covered in this chapter, to help you find news stories and how to decide whether or not a news article is true. Hopefully, you will use some of the websites you learned about in this chapter to read some of today's news.

Vocabulary

traditional	bias	format
digital	point of view	breaking news
blog	editorial	podcasts
knowledgable	cover	controversial

Idioms

word of mouth	bearer of bad news
break the news	get the lowdown
hot off the press	bad news travels fast
no news is good news	keep me posted
that's news to me	heard it through the grapevine
get up to speed	

Do you remember all of the information covered in this chapter? If not, go back and review it to make sure you do. Practice the vocabulary and idioms in your conversations, and look for them when reading different materials. Make sure to use the websites provided to check if the news you read today is true! Also look for other websites that you might like to use regularly to keep up with the news.

ANSWER KEY

CHAPTER 1

TRUE OR FALSE

1. TRUE
2. FALSE
3. TRUE
4. TRUE
5. FALSE
6. TRUE
7. TRUE
8. FALSE
9. FALSE
10. TRUE

VOCABULARY CROSSWORD

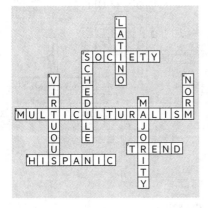

STORY TIME

1. C
2. D
3. A
4. A
5. A

WRITE IT DOWN

1. A culture vulture is someone who is very interested in the arts.
2. No, she is not a culture vulture.
3. (Answers will vary.)
4. (Answers will vary.)

MATCHING

1. E
2. F
3. H
4. J
5. A
6. I
7. L
8. N
9. B
10. C
11. D
12. G
13. K
14. M

CHAPTER 2

IDIOM AND VOCABULARY CROSSWORD

STOP AND THINK

1. ice
2. cheesy
3. nuts
4. piece
5. pie
6. icing
7. cake
8. cherry
9. feeds
10. eggs
11. chicken

DIALOGUE 3

Idioms and Vocabulary words: cheesy, cold as ice, two peas in a pod, going nuts, a piece of cake, the icing on the cake

MATCHING

1. B
2. A
3. N
4. E
5. G
6. I
7. K
8. C
9. L
10. F
11. H
12. J
13. D
14. M

CHAPTER 3

STORY TIME

1. B
2. A
3. A
4. B
5. B

DIALOGUE 2

Idioms and Vocabulary words: Overcook, seasoning, ingredients, indulge, cooking up a storm

MATCHING

1. H
2. C
3. G
4. D
5. J
6. F
7. E
8. I
9. B
10. A

IDIOM CROSSWORD

CHAPTER 4

TRUE OR FALSE

1. TRUE
2. FALSE
3. FALSE
4. TRUE
5. FALSE
6. TRUE
7. FALSE

VOCABULARY CROSSWORD 1

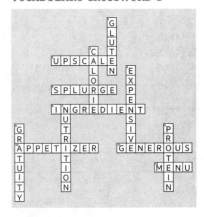

MATCHING

1. B
2. C
3. H
4. F
5. M
6. K
7. E
8. L
9. A
10. G
11. J
12. I
13. D

STOP AND THINK

1. spot
2. hatch
3. cheese
4. nines
5. salt
6. chicken
7. oven
8. turkey
9. joe
10. on
11. sky
12. hand

VOCABULARY CROSSWORD 2

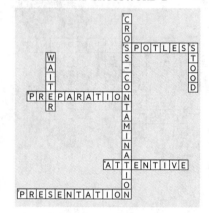

STORY TIME

1. They did not have enough money to go out to dinner for a pizza and to a movie theater.
2. They got takeout pizza and watched a movie at home. Sofia also brought popcorn.

CHAPTER 5

TRUE OR FALSE

1. TRUE
2. FALSE
3. TRUE
4. TRUE
5. TRUE
6. TRUE
7. FALSE
8. FALSE
9. TRUE
10. TRUE
11. TRUE

STORY TIME

1. B
2. C
3. B
4. A
5. C

DIALOGUE 2

Vocabulary words: credit card, online
Idioms: money to burn, cost a pretty penny, bank on it

IDIOM CROSSWORD

DIALOGUE 3

8 idioms

CHAPTER 6

MATCHING

1. B
2. E
3. J
4. D
5. A
6. C
7. F
8. G
9. I
10. H

VOCABULARY CROSSWORD

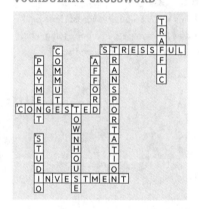

STOP AND THINK: FILL IN THE BLANKS

1. He tries not to see his cousin when he visits town. He tries to keep someone at a distance.
2. In order to buy or rent a house you need to have money. It's all about the Benjamins.
3. He accepted the job instead of waiting to see if he had other job offers because a bird in the hand is worth two in the bush.
4. It is so much easier to buy a house if you have money saved. That is because money makes the world go round.
5. Sofia loves being at home because home is where the heart is.
6. She is going to keep trying even if it takes her a month to find the perfect place to live. She is going the distance.

IDIOM AND VOCABULARY CROSSWORD

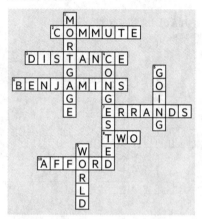

CHAPTER 7

TRUE OR FALSE

1. FALSE
2. FALSE
3. FALSE
4. TRUE
5. FALSE

MATCHING

1. C
2. F
3. H
4. G
5. A
6. B
7. D
8. E

STORY TIME

1. C
2. D
3. A
4. B

STOP AND THINK

1. maintenance
2. thermostat
3. landscaping
4. technology
5. grounds
6. fertilizing
7. HVAC
8. contemporary
9. siding
10. resident
11. walk-through
12. circuit

IDIOM CROSSWORD

CHAPTER 8

STOP AND THINK 1

1. résumé
2. opportunities
3. format
4. templates
5. edit
6. firsthand

VOCABULARY CROSSWORD

STOP AND THINK 2

1. All in a day's work
2. Work against the clock
3. Dirty work
4. Do your homework
5. Work your fingers to the bone
6. Works for me
7. Work through something
8. Busy work
9. Worked up
10. Works like magic

STORY TIME

1. C
2. B
3. C
4. B

IDIOM CROSSWORD

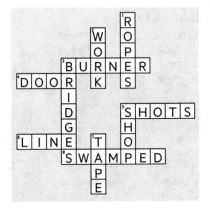

DIALOGUE 3: VOCABULARY AND IDIOMS

Idioms and Vocabulary words:
opportunities, Monster, Indeed,
LinkedIn, firsthand

CHAPTER 9

TRUE OR FALSE

1. FALSE
2. TRUE
3. TRUE
4. FALSE
5. TRUE
6. TRUE
7. FALSE
8. TRUE
9. TRUE

VOCABULARY CROSSWORD

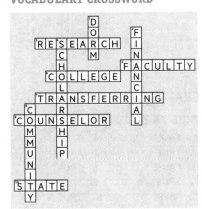

STOP AND THINK

1. transferring
2. touch
3. college
4. track
5. institution
6. community

MATCHING

1. D
2. G
3. A
4. E
5. C
6. F
7. B
8. I
9. H

CHAPTER 10

TRUE OR FALSE

1. TRUE
2. FALSE
3. TRUE
4. FALSE
5. TRUE
6. TRUE
7. TRUE
8. FALSE
9. FALSE
10. TRUE

MATCHING

1. C
2. A
3. B
4. D
5. E
6. F
7. G

STOP AND THINK

1. partner
2. pay
3. run
4. hot
5. steal
6. sorry
7. murder
8. robbery
9. bars
10. something
11. easy
12. music
13. book

STORY TIME

1. A
2. B
3. C
4. B
5. A

DIALOGUE 2

crime doesn't pay; still on the run; behind
bars; an ounce of prevention is worth a
pound of cure; 4 idioms

GUESS THE IDIOM

1. Hand in the cookie jar—stealing
   money
2. Serve time—spend time in jail or
   prison

STOP AND THINK

Idioms and Vocabulary words: a steal;
surroundings; a hot car

CHAPTER 11

TRUE OR FALSE

1. TRUE
2. TRUE
3. TRUE
4. TRUE
5. FALSE
6. TRUE
7. TRUE
8. FALSE
9. TRUE

VOCABULARY CROSSWORD

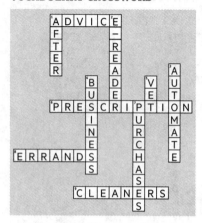

IDIOMS

1. burn the candle at both ends—someone that is working too hard, getting up early and staying up late to work
2. taskmaster—someone who not only gives work to others, but is bothering them about completing the work all of the time
3. to break even—to have no money left because the amount of money you made was spent
4. Jack of all trades—a person who is good at doing many things
5. back to the grind—getting back to work
6. break your back—doing a lot of work
7. last resort—the last thing you are going to try; for example, going to one more store to find your favorite socks
8. sail through—doing something easily
9. take it easy—doing things at a slow pace
10. pain in the neck—something or someone that is annoying

STOP AND THINK

1. grind
2. Jack
3. ends
4. last
5. sail
6. easy
7. taskmaster
8. break
9. back

STORY TIME

1. A
2. C
3. B
4. B
5. B

CHAPTER 12

TRUE OR FALSE

1. FALSE
2. TRUE
3. TRUE
4. TRUE
5. TRUE
6. TRUE
7. FALSE

STORY TIME

1. A
2. B
3. C
4. B

STOP AND THINK

1. rains
2. weather
3. warm
4. storm
5. calm
6. cloud
7. dogs
8. fair
9. check
10. thunder

DIALOGUE 2

2 idioms

VOCABULARY CROSSWORD

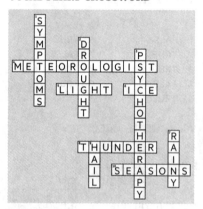

CHAPTER 13

TRUE OR FALSE

1. TRUE
2. TRUE
3. FALSE
4. TRUE
5. FALSE
6. TRUE
7. FALSE
8. TRUE
9. TRUE
10. TRUE

MATCHING

1. B
2. F
3. A
4. E
5. C
6. G
7. D
8. H

IDIOM CROSSWORD

STORY TIME

1. B
2. C
3. C
4. A
5. C

DIALOGUE 2

Idioms: there's no place like home; kick back

CHAPTER 14

VOCABULARY CROSSWORD

MATCHING

1. D, G
2. B
3. C, F
4. E
5. A

IDIOM CROSSWORD

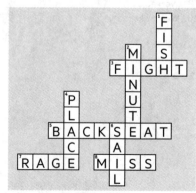

STOP AND THINK

Interjections: Hello, Yeah, Hmm, awesome, aww

Idioms: on the home stretch, falling into place

STORY TIME

1. C
2. A
3. A
4. C
5. D

CHAPTER 15

TRUE OR FALSE

1. TRUE
2. TRUE
3. TRUE
4. FALSE
5. TRUE
6. FALSE
7. TRUE

VOCABULARY CROSSWORD

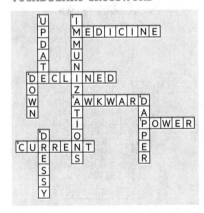

MATCHING

1. A
2. D
3. B
4. E
5. F
6. C

STOP AND THINK

1. move
2. ship
3. ride
4. board
5. suitcase
6. bus
7. fly
8. overboard
9. ways

STORY TIME

1. C
2. A
3. B
4. A
5. C

CHAPTER 16

STOP AND THINK 1

1. landscaping
2. assistance
3. research
4. opportunities
5. organizations
6. videography
7. Immigrants
8. volunteer
9. forward
10. therapy

VOCABULARY CROSSWORD

STORY TIME

1. A
2. C
3. B
4. C
5. A

STOP AND THINK 2

1. shoulders
2. cross
3. bridges
4. minds
5. boat
6. friend
7. birds
8. two's
9. high
10. language
11. indeed
12. halfway
13. page
14. circles

DIALOGUE 2

IDIOMS

4: friends in high places, meeting of the minds, birds of a feather, build bridges

VOCABULARY

5: gathering, volunteer, research, organization, embarrassed

CHAPTER 17

MATCHING

1. I
2. J
3. C
4. A
5. D
6. F
7. H
8. G
9. E
10. B

TRUE OR FALSE

1. FALSE
2. TRUE
3. FALSE
4. TRUE
5. TRUE
6. FALSE
7. FALSE
8. TRUE

IDIOM CROSSWORD

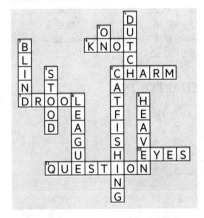

STORY TIME

1. A
2. A
3. B
4. C
5. C

CHAPTER 18

STOP AND THINK

1. selections
2. pay
3. concession
4. 3-D
5. subscribe
6. IMAX
7. replicate
8. 4-D
9. audience
10. premiere

MATCHING

1. B
2. F
3. A
4. E
5. C
6. D
7. I
8. H
9. G
10. J

IDIOM CROSSWORD

STORY TIME

1. C   4. C
2. B   5. C
3. A

TRUE or FALSE

1. TRUE   6. TRUE
2. FALSE   7. TRUE
3. TRUE   8. TRUE
4. TRUE   9. FALSE
5. FALSE   10. FALSE

CHAPTER 19

MATCHING

1. C   5. B
2. D   6. G
3. F   7. E
4. A

WRITE IT DOWN 2

1. Be careful about what you post.
2. Be careful not to spend too much time on social media.

TRUE OR FALSE

1. FALSE   4. FALSE
2. TRUE   5. TRUE
3. FALSE   6. TRUE

STOP AND THINK 1

1. cyberspace   4. curve
2. following   5. viral
3. net   6. science

STOP AND THINK 2

1. Twitter
2. Facebook or Instagram
3. Facebook or Instagram
4. Facebook or Instagram
5. Facebook or Instagram
6. Twitter

STORY TIME

1. It is usually quiet in Juan's room.
2. His room was a mess.
3. He didn't want to learn about another website.
4. You can look for information or ideas about how to do things.

VOCABULARY CROSSWORD

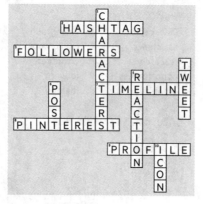

CHAPTER 20

STOP AND THINK 1

1. documentaries   6. PayPal
2. subscriptions   7. trailers
3. launch   8. consumer
4. classic   9. premium
5. upload   10. rate

MATCHING

1. B   4. A
2. E   5. F
3. C   6. D

TRUE OR FALSE

1. FALSE   4. TRUE
2. FALSE   5. TRUE
3. TRUE   6. TRUE

STOP AND THINK 2

1. blue   4. practice
2. long   5. whistles
3. button   6. wheel

VOCABULARY CROSSWORD

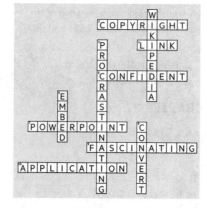

CHAPTER 21

WRITE IT DOWN

Traditional sources are on paper (and may also be online), such as newspapers and magazines. However, digital sources are only online, such as websites, news feeds, and blogs.

STOP AND THINK 1

1. traditional   5. knowledgeable
2. editorial   6. digital
3. cover   7. point
4. bias   8. speed

MATCHING

1. C   4. A
2. D   5. E
3. B

VOCABULARY CROSSWORD

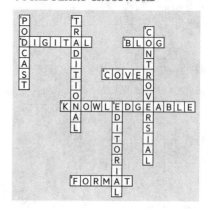

STORY TIME

1. B   4. A
2. D   5. B
3. D

STOP AND THINK 2

1. word   6. press
2. me   7. bad
3. good   8. posted
4. break   9. lowdown
5. bearer   10. grapevine

INDEX